RADICAL PARENTING

SEVEN STEPS TO A FUNCTIONAL FAMILY
IN A DYSFUNCTIONAL WORLD

BY

BRAD BLANTON, PH.D.

Author of

Radical Honesty

and

Practicing Radical Honesty

and

Honest to God (with Neale Donald Walsch)

Published by:
Sparrowhawk Publications
646 Shuler Lane
Stanley, VA 22851
800 EL TRUTH
www.radicalhonesty.com

Distributed by:
Hampton Roads Publishing
1125 Stony Ridge Road
Charlottesville, VA 22902
Orders: 800.766.8009

© 2002 Brad Blanton

Produced by Author's Publishing Cooperative
Cover by Vicki Valentine
Interior Design by Art Squad Graphics
Printed in USA
First Edition

10 9 8 7 6 5 4 3 2 1

This book is dedicated to Elijah Forest Blanton, my teacher,
whom I love with all of my heart.

*"The ultimate attainment of adulthood is to re-accomplish
that seriousness of a child at play."*

FRIEDRICH NEITZCHE

RADICAL PARENTING
SEVEN STEPS TO A FUNCTIONAL FAMILY IN A DYSFUNCTIONAL WORLD

TABLE OF CONTENTS

WHO I AM AND WHY I AM WRITING THIS BOOK

THIS BOOK IS THE THIRD I have written as a result of observing, studying, thinking about and discussing the war between being and mind first discussed in *Radical Honesty; How To Transform Your Life By Telling The Truth* (Dell, 1995), and elaborated on in a second book, *Practicing Radical Honesty: How To Complete the Past, Live in the Present and Build a Future With a Little Help from Your Friends* (Sparrowhawk, 2001). I have been working on this book for years, even while writing those other books. I have long wanted to write a book on parenting, based on a lifetime of watching how a mind gets built, how it functions, and how it malfunctions.

After all these years of working closely as a psychotherapist with people who were screwed up by how they were parented, instructed, and acculturated, I am asking, and attempting to answer, a question that grows out of a central set of assumptions. These assumptions are:

(1) The primary cause of stress is the mind of the individual suffering from stress.

(2) Attachment to the ideals and ideas of the mind, which sources stress, includes attachment to the ideal of who we are.

(3) Almost all of us lie about who we are and what we've done and what we think and feel, regularly and habitually, in order to create a good impression and maintain our image of ourselves, the way our culture encourages us to do.

(4) Lying keeps us trapped in the jail of our minds.

(5) Because of being in our minds, so preoccupied with our image and our performance, we are removed from our experience and unable to come in contact with, and be nurtured by, other people.

The question based on those assumptions is: Is there a way to parent children so that this kind of suffering can be avoided? That is the central question around which this book is organized.

Out of that question these others arise:

- What kind of treatment and environment to grow up in makes people happy and free?

- How might one design a way for children to be raised so that they don't have to suffer so much as adolescents and adults?

- Is there a way to raise children, right from the beginning, so that they don't become so lost in their minds?

- Could the whole period of the growth of the mind in childhood and adolescence be designed and nurtured in a more functional way than we have generally done so far?

- What would parenting and education look like if child-rearing could be focused entirely on bringing about the balanced use of the mind, while remaining centered in the experience of being in the body?

- Why couldn't people just start out playing, curious and happy, and continue that way as they grow, and grow and grow?
- What are the most commonsense, easiest, most functional, most efficient ways to treat children as they unfold? How can we assist them in the task of growing, not get in their way and still have them turn out all right?
- How can we use the benefits of, but at the same time transcend, the limitations of our constrained cultural view and raise our children so they are not as screwed up as we are?

I think the key to answering these questions is in growing up ourselves, a little more than most of us have. I think that transcending our own childhood experiences by getting over our reactions to how we were treated by our own parents is critical. I think that is what allows us to choose how we raise our own children. Of course, that is not enough. We also have to get over the limitations of the larger family we were born into, called a culture. If we really love our children and want them to be happy and contribute to the well-being of people and the world, we have to transcend more than our little personal dysfunctional family—we have to get over the big dysfunctional family's limitations as well. The big dysfunctional family problem is a primary consideration for how to raise kids. Those of us who have suffered from—and understand—the limitations of the culture in which we were raised, want to consciously correct the cultural presuppositions we learned to believe that caused our suffering, rather than pass that suffering on to our children.

MY EXPERIENCE AS A PARENT

I have been a significant participant in the raising of five children, one in each decade since the 1950s. I was nine years old when my youngest brother was born. My mother had four miscarriages caused by my stepfather's beating her. Mike was born early, also after a beating, and survived. I was his primary caretaker from his birth in 1949 until early in his fifth year in 1953. Our family, headed by drunks who were themselves children, eventually broke up as a result of many events, including my twelve-year-old-brother and I fracturing my stepfather's skull, and breaking three of his ribs, before leaving home. After that therapeutic event, and a few more like it with my stepfather—and sixteen years of psychotherapy—I'm almost over having my reactions to how I was parented completely run my life.

Though I was only nine years old when my youngest brother was born, I loved him with all my heart. When I was thirteen years old the family broke up. After they had fallen behind three months on the house payments, I stole the money for the payment needed to avoid having the house repossessed, and refused to return it. I told my stepfather and mother, when they were sober, that unless they agreed to my terms unconditionally, I would kill him. Under those conditions we "negotiated" an agreement that my little brother would move in with his grandmother and stay nearby in Virginia. My next brother, who was twelve years old, would move to Tennessee with an aunt and uncle, and I would go to live with my adult sister and brother-in-law in Texas. Even though I was the one primarily responsible for that solution, when we separated and dispersed to our various locations, I felt like I had lost my child and my little brother felt like he had lost his father. Mike is fifty years old now and I am fifty-nine. We still love and support each other as adults, but that gap that was created by our separation has never completely closed for either one of us.

When I was seventeen, my girlfriend in Texas got pregnant; we married the day after I turned eighteen. We separated and the marriage was annulled before the baby was born, and the child was given up for adoption in Florida at the Florence Crittenden home for unwed mothers. I have never seen that son and took no responsibility for his upbringing. So my first complete failure as a parent also occurred in the 1950s.

I had a daughter in 1968, when I was twenty-eight years old. When her mother and I divorced after ten years of marriage, Shanti was almost four. Though I had her with me during summers and holidays, after she and her mother moved to California and I stayed in Washington, D.C., I couldn't be with her for months at a time, and I felt like I lost Shanti at a young age just like I had lost my brother Mike when I was thirteen. I was responsible for the separations in both cases but managed to remain feeling like a victim nevertheless. I imagine my poor pathetic reactive mind created that loss so I could do a better job of staying in contact when we got separated than I had done the first time I lost a child. The first thirty-five years of my life were run by my reactive mind and rationalized by my linear mind, without much knowledge of what was going on, on my part, as I believe happens with most people. I was trying to "do" that first loss over and over again until I got it right. I didn't get it right but I did it a little better. Shanti and I had some hard times but we came through okay. She is thirty-three now and very successful and we are close and still love and support each other as adults.

Then came my son, Amos, in 1975, born of my next wife, Joanie. His mother and I divorced also, but have co-parented well and stayed in the same territory and worked together in his raising, and I didn't have to lose him except for his growing up, which is an inevitable loss that comes with parenthood, as a part of the package. I learned with him, and from him, that growing up itself is full of losses and abandonments—regardless of how hard we try to keep them from happening. He is twenty-six and has graduated from college and is working now and headed back to graduate school. He is quite a comedian and a very good man, and we still love and support each other as adults.

In 1985, from my fourth, most recent marriage, my daughter Carson was born. This writing is the morning of her fourteenth birthday, and she is helping some with this book by the way she has taught us how wonderfully she can learn just by being supported in her curiosity. She was the first child that my wife and I had the sense not to force into some stupid curriculum, based on outmoded concepts, about what her path of learning should be. Her mother, Amy, and I are separated now, but still friends and raising our two children together. We lived together for twenty-two years. We live near each other and still co-parent consciously with a lot of help from our friends. We are home schooling Carsie and vice versa. Amy is very close to Shanti and Amos as well and they have loved their sister wonderfully since her birth.

In 1993 our son Elijah was born. His sister Carsie is helping with his life schooling, and she gets some help in that from Shanti and Amos and Amy and me. We all love each other and do a pretty good job of familying.

Amy and I were both raised to think that people are supposed to stay together for life when they get married, and declared when we formed that union that we would. But, as many others have discovered, it doesn't always turn out that way. In fact, it usually doesn't, doesn't have to, and still often works out okay—just not according to the model we attempt to impose on ourselves about the way things ought to be.

The odds are your kids and mine will be married and divorced several times. We can be okay with that. It is just a change from one model about how we are supposed to do it to another model of how to do it. We can still do a good job of parenting, however, even if we separate, and Amy and I have.

I was the biological father of another child, Ian, in the 1970s. I didn't find out I was his father until he was fourteen years old when his mother sued me for child support. I gave blood and so did he and it turned out she was right, I was his father. I supported him financially then, for the next seven years until he was twenty-one, but didn't see him much and didn't have anything to do with parenting him. He met me and his brother Amos and sisters Shanti and Carsie when he was still in his teens. After he turned twenty-one his mother and he left town and went, I think, to her parents' home in England and we haven't heard from them since. My only parenting of him consisted of telling him the truth about my relationship with his mother in the early '70s and my numerous sexual and drug exploits at the time. Another failure on my part, I think, and I am sorry for how I handled that as well.

So I have been the biological father of six children in the last five decades and the responsible parent of five, one of whom was my brother and not my biological child. Amy and I also had charge of two nephews for a couple of years in the early '90s as well. I learned a lot from loving them and succeeding and failing with them.

I expect for the next few decades to be grandfathering and to continue my education in childrearing. I think, so far, I have done a better job with each child, as I grew older. I have learned from many successes and many mistakes. But I am happy to be able to say this: Because of my children, and in spite of my own stupidity, I have been in love all of my life.

Nothing whatsoever in my entire life has been more powerful than that complete and willing presence and reverberating love of children who were themselves loved. I have loved my children without any qualifications. I find loving children really easy to do and I think most people who are not completely lost in their minds do. I find I can love adults and even teenagers sometimes the same way, and usually it is when I get a peek at the child within.

Many wonderful children have taught me important things by the way they loved me back. It is out of that love I have received from children of all ages that I am writing this book. Somehow I took more direction from love than from tradition. What I have learned works, not perfectly, but probably much more reliably than the advice from the usual so-called expert authority. Someone who successfully resides obliviously within the context of a sick society, in which control and money are the primary considerations of value, is probably less to be trusted than myself.

I have helped adults in psychotherapy for over twenty-five years to get over the ravages of middle-class child abuse. I am indebted to these people who were poisoned by their parents and teachers in the name of education "for their own good." These people have taught me how not to raise children. My own experience of being loved and listened to over the course of my own personal sixteen years of psychotherapy and training and workshops has allowed me to speak now as a recovering child.

WHAT CHILDREN GET CALLED FORTH INTO

Little beings get called forth into a culture, and so far, our culture, is usually not a pretty picture. The way children are birthed and raised in our culture contrasts directly with a vision many of us in my current family and community share as a possibility. We see that there is a real possibility for a fulfilling and happy lifetime of play and service for every human being on the planet. We can invite these little beings into a lifetime of play and service, by playing with them and serving them.

Out of this, and only out of this, will occur the reorganization of the world into a more nurturing place for human beings. We can raise our children in such a way that we bring about the end of culturally-endorsed child abuse by modeling the alternative. This will bring about even greater results in the world, once compassionate parents and children act in the larger world based on what they have learned from each other.

Child-rearing is of critical importance to the maintenance of all our cultural dysfunctions. Changes in child-rearing practices are likewise critical to healing our dysfunctions. Bringing about the end of starvation on the planet, the reestablishment of ecological balance, the end of the military industrial complex, nuclear disarmament, the

end of the "war on drugs," factionalism, racism, top down management, war, the beginning of a more compassionate economic order—
all these could flow from a new social honoring of our fundamental
love for our children and of each other as older children.

I live in a community of friends. They help me with everything I
do, including this book. We hope this book will help you a lot in raising your kids and having fun doing it, attentively, playfully and in no
hurry, casually saving the world from human beings, and human beings from themselves.

HUMAN BEINGS, THE DEPRIVATION-BASED SPECIES: THE SOCIOBIOLOGICAL PERSPECTIVE

IS THERE A PERSPECTIVE THAT transcends all cultural perspectives? Is it possible to use a perspective that transcends our culture to helpfully inform us about how to raise our children to be in—but not of—our limited cultural set? I think we can do that. Let's start by taking a much longer view in time, starting way back before the teeny little blip in time known as the twentieth century.

About seven million years ago the stream that separated us from our first cousins the chimpanzees began flowing right for us and left for them. The mere 1.6% difference in our genetic makeup accounts for our having taken over the world and their having survived in smaller numbers. Small changes manifested in big differences not only in the numbers of each species that survived and prospered, but also in the way we behaved. The capacities we evolved from our slowly modifying genetic evolution, eventually resulted in the invention of language by children about 50,000 years ago. Amy Silver (*Guerilla Learning,* Wiley, 2001) says that little children, in playgroups, invented language. This time period was what Jared Diamond calls "the great leap forward" when we really began to modify tools and our environment, organize hunts, and eventually domesticate animals for work.

The most striking feature of human infancy and childhood is its duration. The premature beginning all humans have was as a result of a few evolutionary changes. The combination of our upright posture and big heads (because of big brains) apparently required that the babies exit earlier from the womb if they were not to grow too big to get out at all (see Elaine Morgan, *The Descent of the Child*). So we have had a radical departure from our forbears in how prematurely our babies are born. Human babies are essentially born in a fetal state. Since our infants come prematurely and are helpless for so long a time, it is impossible for them not to be mishandled.

We have evolved such that there is a continuum of growth from conception to two years of age, during which the greatest amount of learning occurs and the greatest need for care exists. Throughout human history at least two adults were required to care for and feed the infant during this time in order for it to survive. The probability of survival was enhanced by living in family groups or tribes.

None of the parenting pairs throughout our history of being born too early ever did a very good job, compared to the job done by nature when infants of other species are born. Newborns of most big mammal species are usually fully able to take care of themselves at birth or become so in a matter of hours, or at most a few weeks. From birth, humans have this hard-wired, guaranteed inadequacy of care of their young. Everyone in modern times who has tried to meet a baby's every need knows how impossible it is to do so, no matter how much you love them and how hard you try. Imagine how much more impossible that would be in a cave with bad water and nothing much to eat and occasional visits by creatures who want to eat you.

Out of that situation our intellects developed more and more, perhaps related to our desperately trying to survive, and our yearning to become whole and in love again, like we remembered from the womb and the first few months after being born. Eventually, out of our separation from our mothers and yearning for wholeness, we came up with many useful adaptations and new learnings. We also came up with some hateful, mean and merciless adaptations, concerning dominating the environment and other creatures, and others of our own kind. We developed, out of our extended and frequent deprivation at a helpless stage of being, a yearning and a hunger for a wholeness we could still barely intuitively remember from our time in the womb and our time next to Mama's body, nursing. We kept losing touch with this sense of the wholeness and unity of things, this sense of rightness, with no power to bring it about again.

Along with, and maybe out of, this tremendous yearning came, over time, two important ways of surviving that differed radically from our chimpanzee cousins. We changed how we did sex, and we changed how much we fought to take care of ourselves.

We changed how we did sex so we could all do it all the time whether the female was ovulating or not. We changed how we took care of ourselves, compensating for years of helplessness by grasping, fighting, taking, becoming merciless killers, capturers, tamers, users, territory protectors, and the meanest of all species on the earth.

Nature designed a life that gets us deprived a lot and hurts more for a long time at a tender age than any other life it has ever designed. That life is the life of Homo sapiens. More than any other life of any other species, we frequently lose what we depend on and cherish. And we remember both the bliss that preceded the loss and the loss itself better than any other creature that has ever lived before.

You and I were born to be inadequate. We were born inadequately prepared for life. We were inadequately cared for when we were young. We were born to come up short and yearn for a vague memory of when we had a dawning consciousness of wholeness. This is not just our story, not just you and me in this time. It is the story of the human race. (So remember this, when you're giving yourself hell in your own mind for not being good enough, or not being a good enough parent: If God had wanted to have your babies cared for perfectly from the beginning, she would have made you a horse.)

Chimpanzees live in groups and must also care for their young for a more extended period than other species, but except for being 98.4% exactly like us in genetic makeup, they are nothing like us. When a female is ovulating she goes into heat. Her buttocks become swollen and change to a rosy red and she emits odors that attract males. All the males that are strong enough to fend off the other males have sex with her until she is no longer in heat. After she stops ovulating, she is no longer interesting to them. Her "display" of sight and smell has many parallels in other species; signalling the male for fertilization only when he is needed is an old story.

Humans evolved another strategy. The human females became permanently "in display," with their rounded breasts and buttocks signaling readiness at all times. Men were constantly signalled to mate and fight off other males who also wanted to mate with the same appealing female. So the males, of this most driven of all species, are even more tortured than females, as they struggle to meet the built-in biochemical demands of their bodies for sex, food, drugs and rock and roll. They mostly just remain dissatisfied forever. Nature figured if we just had sex all the time, kind of like plants, only with a hell of a lot more trouble, we would have good odds of having sex during ovulation. The sperm would be there when the egg came down the tube. So that's how we do it. We are the only mammals who developed concealed ovulation. It worked. There are many more of us than there are chimps.

It's no wonder then that the second clear difference between chimpanzees and us is in aggressiveness. No other species even comes close to the viciousness of the males of our species. Our males will kill off completely any other species that is defenseless against them, just for a steak now and then. We also kill off all the men, women and children of any other groups we consider different and threatening. Successful and unsuccessful attempts at total genocide go way back past recorded history to inferred history based on archeological data. Our males have killed whatever human beings they came across, without any hesitation to speak of, as long as we have had the capacity to develop a category with which to label them as enemy. We are merciless murderers (including, some believe, the killing off of our vegetarian counterparts, the Neanderthals). Women and children who can't be captured and used get killed as mercilessly as the male enemies. Likewise the pets, livestock and slaves all get killed, the whole village burned, and all possessions taken or destroyed.

We're humans. We fornicate and fight all the time. We kill and we fornicate. We're never satisfied. And we take it out on our enemies. What happened to the Jews in Nazi Germany, the American Indians, Australian Aborigines, Bosnians and Muslims was not unique. A modern businessman is reputed to have said, "Yea, though I walk through the valley of the shadow of death, I shall fear no evil . . . because I'm the meanest sonofabitch in the valley!" This is a clear articulation of one of the primary reasons we have been successful in taking over the earth. In the words of marines and sailors returning from the Pacific front after World War Two, in their arrogance after having won the largest murdering contest in history: "Fuck, fight or run! Win, lose or draw!" We are, without a doubt, the meanest species on the planet.

Relatively recently, just this very last second in evolutionary time, we have developed a way to escape some of the suffering. While we were developing our desperate survival capacities, we became alienated from the experience of life, the life of feeling and sensation. We developed the capacity to be alienated from our experience. Our neocortex grew large enough to rival our limbic brain. Out of deep dissatisfaction with the life we were designed for, we developed intellect. We, as a species, learned how to dissociate. When circumstances became unbearable we learned how to "go to Carolina in our minds." By systematically spacing out when circumstances became too painful, we extended our limited intellectual ability and developed the mind.

From this long history of pain comes our wisdom, our compassion, our ferocity and our ability to inflict further pain. Our material advancement and scientific progress—as well as the incredible depths of our ignorance—are generated by our intellects in the ungrounded space of our alienation from being itself.

After a few hundred millennia of senseless murder, some of us discovered meditation. It allowed us to notice our groundedness in being. And it's much easier than conquering the world. Oops! Too bad we didn't notice that earlier. Now we have to start over, based on that less miserable way to live, and reorganize the world again.

Fortunately, we *can* rewrite the software. But we have to get on it right away. We have to start with a new relationship to our own minds, and a rearranged way of treating our children that is truly conscious and not interfered with by unexamined poisonous cultural habits.

How can we keep the advantage of intellect but do away with the suffering of alienation? The answer, according to Jean Liedloff, who spent years in the deep Amazonian jungles with a hunter-gatherer culture to discover this, is in *recontacting experience:* "In all who, for a time, hand over the reins of the intellect to unthinking being, the cause of greater well-being is served." We *can* be more satisfied. We *can* raise humans who are more satisfiable—even male humans. We *can* raise more satisfied babies, by not tearing them loose so hard and so fast from Mama's feel, from the touch of others, from nursing, from cuddling, from being handed from one person to another.

We evolved so we had to get born too early or not at all. That is the source of our wonderful wisdom, tremendous suffering and incredible ignorance. How lucky can one species get? There are over six billion of us now. How unlucky can one species get?

It may be possible to use the same intelligence that got us into this dilemma to get us out of it. Unlikely, but possible. If we learn to care we have a chance. The perspective from which this book is written is a kind of all-inclusive caring, called compassion. It evolved recently among humans whose heart-relatedness to their children led them to love and honor being.

We are constantly giving birth to new teachers. We fail to learn from them when we block what they have to teach us with the idea that they are inferior to us because we are adults. Therefore, this book is designed to interfere with our blocks to learning from them. This may be our only hope for survival as a species.

There are seven steps for parents to take to arrive at a state of openness that allows adult human beings and new human beings to learn mutually from each other and nourish each other as a family. Parents who want to create functional families can do so by:

(1) Completing what has been incomplete in their own lives, particularly with their own parents;

(2) Forgiving their dysfunctional culture;

(3) Gaining a new perspective on being a human being that transcends their culture;

(4) Coming to a clear understanding of how the brain and mind work;

(5) Learning how to create creators by not blocking creativity;

(6) Getting good at envisioning possibilities; and

(7) Integrating and applying what they have learned from outgrowing their parents and their culture.

That's all there is to it. All you have to do is grow up and at the same time never get over being a child.

1 THROW OUT THE BATHWATER, KEEP THE BABY

THE EXPRESSION "DON'T THROW OUT the baby with the bathwater!" comes from medieval times. In those days, folks only took baths a couple of times a year. On "bath day" one tub of water was heated up and the men of the house got to go first, then the women, then the older children, and last of all the babies. By the time the babies got in the bath the water was so dirty you couldn't see them in it, so you had to remember not to "throw out the baby with the bathwater." I like to run that analogy into the ground by saying that there is a lot of dirty water we can't see our babies for, and we have to throw it out and see the baby.

The seven steps this book is organized around are hard work, and understanding why you might take the risk of doing those steps is heavy sledding too. There is a lot of negative reassessment of things we have all been taught to value, particularly in the beginning of the beginning. I cuss now and then and use other offensive language, although we have cleaned it up quite a bit from the way I usually talk. It doesn't get fun or funny enough until near the end.

If, when you finish the book, you want your money back we won't give it to you, but you can burn the book. Please hang in there a while even if you get offended, we have to throw out of the bathwater first in order to keep the baby.

A STANDARD BY WHICH WE CAN MEASURE MODERN EDUCATIONAL SYSTEMS AND CHILD-REARING PRACTICES

Explanations are not reality. Explanations are interpretations of reality. All explanations are bullshit, but some are more useful than others. We have to remember the difference between bullshit and reality at all times, in order to remain grounded once we've gone sane. Try out the explanations I review of evolutionists, biochemists, theoreticians of child development and learning and the ones I make up myself. Substitute this bunch of theories for the bunch of theories you were raised on and with and try them on for size. All these theories are just models to work from and none of them are true. The ones I have to offer, I say, are a hell of a lot better than the ones you were raised with.

I have had a lot of help and a lot of information from other people in writing this book. We all use in common this general rule of thumb to judge and compare theories about how to treat children: The ones that cover the most information and that explain the most amount of data are the best ones. Even though all explanations and standards are just more bullshit from the mind, some work better than others. Usefulness and comprehensiveness are our primary standards to go by when we are using our minds to abstract from experience.

WHO THIS BOOK IS FOR

If you are a parent or intend to be one soon, or a grandparent who is interested in helping do it differently than you did the first time, read this book and pass it on. The possibility of health and happiness for our children and grandchildren depends upon our ability to transcend belief and to help our children learn to transcend belief over and over again. The reformation of parenting as a means to transcend provincial cultural belief is up to us.

Human ignorance is unbounded, mostly because the intellect can so easily get carried away with itself and ignore the data of commonsense experience. Often the education children receive from parents and teachers instills this kind of ignorance in them. They learn to ignore their experience and become overly attached to belief. Those damaged by attachment to belief I call moralists. Moralists for some reason tend to become preachers and teachers and parents. They advocate that children lose touch with their senses and focus on their minds' provincial cultural ideals and beliefs, thus completing the cycle of ignorance.

This over attachment to belief as a substitute for awareness of commonplace experience is a kind of insanity. The healing of our commonly shared insanity will come from re-grounding ourselves in our senses so we can have a place to stand. Standing here, we may notice we have all gone crazy together. I know this from helping people do it and doing it for myself, repeatedly. All of us were naturally grounded in our senses at birth; we just got trained out of it. We don't have to train our children that way just because it was the way we were trained. We can go back to paying attention rather than buying belief. We can raise our children so they can continue to do what they already do well—pay attention to the world of sensory experience—without being trained out of it.

TRANSCENDING THE CULTURE IN WHICH WE WERE RAISED

I imagine you are a parent, grandparent, foster parent, a caretaker of children, or an adult interested in cultural transcendence. I appreciate you for starting to read this book and for taking your job of taking care of the kids seriously (whether they are your kids or not). I have great empathy for you. I also have a great disrespect for your culture, your mind, your opinions, your beliefs and your probable faith in some other bullshit romantic soap opera daydream.

I imagine that your mind eats on you because of how you were raised. I'm sure you spend a lot of time worrying. You probably spend a lot of your time bothering yourself about not being enough of something or other, the way we've all been taught in our bones by the culture we live in. You may or may not have grown beyond that—but you know that you really want to raise your children differently than you were raised. I am very happy to be writing this book for you, and I hope you get it and I hope you like it and I hope it helps.

After you read this book, if you like it, please come to one of our Radical Parenting workshops. Then help us conduct them.

OTHER BOOKS LIKE RADICAL PARENTING

Before I continue I want to mention a few other books. You may have read some of them already. If you liked any of the following books, you will probably like this one. One of my favorites of all time is *The Continuum Concept* by Jean Liedloff (Perseus, 1986), which has been in print for over twenty years. This book is a masterpiece of comparison of our lives with the lives of people in so-called "primitive" tribes with regard to adult happiness and the parallel child-rearing practices that determine how people turn out in each culture. I have always loved *Summerhill* by A. S. Neill (St. Martin's, 1995), and the books on interest-led learning by John Holt, John Taylor Gatto and Grace Llewellyn. These books are really about the same perspective: hold, touch, love and honor the being of the unfolding little child.

Let them be welcomed into the world to teach you what they need. Watch carefully and learn what they have to teach you out of their interest and natural curiosity and loving you back.

I also like these books: *The War Against Children* by Breggin and Breggin (St. Martin's, 1994); *Spiritual Parenting: A Guide to Understanding and Nurturing Your Child* by Hugh and Gayle Prather (Harmony, 1997); Deepak Chopra's *Seven Spiritual Laws for Parents* (Hyperion, 1998); and Jon Kabat-Zinn's *Everyday Blessings: The Inner Work of Mindful Parenting* (Crown, 1997). These books offer wonderful, caring, insightful guidance for child-rearing, and somewhat transcend the culture into which the authors were born. The book *Love and Survival: The Scientific Basis for the Healing Power of Intimacy* by Dean Ornish, M.D. (HarperCollins, 1997), is pertinent to child-rearing because of its brilliant analysis and evidence of the relationship between wholeness and healing—and the author's clear understanding of the uselessness and damage of moralism without love. Finally, Jared Diamond's *The Third Chimpanzee* (Harper Perennial, 1993), Lewis, Amini and Lannon's book, *A General Theory of Love* (Vintage, 2001) and Pat Love's *Hot Monogamy* (Plume, 1993) are all central to the sociobiological, neuroanatomical, and biochemical perspective which allows us to think outside the limitations our culture has imposed.

If you like Noam Chomsky or David Edwards or Daniel Quinn, or have participated in the "more than consumer" revolution led by Ralph Nader, or believe in the green revolution and the reestablishment of ecological balance, or read the revolutionary evolutionary perspective of Jared Diamond in *Guns, Germs and Steel* (Norton, 1999), or read any novels by Kurt Vonegutt or Tom Robbins or Cormac McCarthy, or liked the movie "American Beauty," or taken part in protesting the issues of racism, war, poverty, or corporate domination over democracy in the course of your lifetime, or done any serious questioning of your own cultural conditioning—this is a book written for you.

You may have thought seriously and talked to your mate and friends about how these things you have come to value or devalue pertain to the rearing of your children. That is a serious conversation. That is the conversation we are going to extend here. I'm as serious as a heart attack about that conversation. This is a very serious book. We've got to get ourselves back to the garden, and our children are the ones to lead us there, and if we can care for them correctly, they will.

ABOUT CONSCIOUSNESS AND CONSCIENTIOUSNESS

This book is for parents who have seen through the limitations of cultural prejudice, and who know firsthand the poverty of moralism and the crippling ignorance of traditional belief. This is for people who wish to start over again—who wish to invent and discover anew what it means for people to live together and create together and love children together. It's for people who are serious about transcending provincial belief and raising their children to know in their bones that they are loved—people who don't think that teaching some set of beliefs about right and wrong is the primary job of parenting. Or, if you are a person who thinks that, and can be open to another view, read on.

This is how *not* to prepare your kids for the rat race. This is a start in thinking for yourself as a parent from a whole new set of assumptions based on something other than moral righteousness about religion, sex, and rock and roll—something other than the ideal of corporate profit, top down management and perennial economic growth as the fundamental sacred presumptions of the right way to live. If you are not one of those people who are pissed off about greed and the destruction of the earth and humanity itself via the various bullshit religious, educational, governmental, industrial and economic institutions from the past that are currently still in power, then you need to clearly identify me and the parents who listen to me. We are the ones who will be stealing your children from you when they grow up.

Conscious child rearing is based on conscious values that transcend unconscious attachment to a cultural subgroup of values based on how we were raised, or in rebellion against how we were raised.

The preservation of consciousness over belief is the most important gift we can give to our children and to humanity. Loving our children unconsciously is not enough. The gift is to love our children consciously with a clear intention to help them stay in touch with the glory of being alive in their bodies as they grow, so they can transcend the jail of their own minds when they grow up. The people in this world are waking up from a long sleep. We can all help. All we have to do is keep each other awake, and not put our children to sleep in the usual way.

Step 1

Completing What Has Been Incomplete in Your Life

2 ⨀ COMPLETING WHAT HAS BEEN INCOMPLETE

We have to start our parenting journey by going through the usually difficult process it takes to forgive our own parents. We need to forgive them for the mistakes they made in their experiments with life, including how they treated us. Then we can at least make new mistakes with our own children, and perhaps less painful ones.

The first step in becoming a good parent is doing some psychological work on yourself that allows you to forgive your own parents. It's best if you don't do this psychological work in a therapist's office. It's best if you do it by talking to your parents, if they are alive. If your parents are dead, then see a therapist or take a trip to the graveyard and do the best you can.

Doing the opposite of what your parents did, in an attempt not to repeat their mistakes is still having the way you treat your own children be dictated by how your parents treated you. If they are alive, they will want to be in on grand parenting and the way they treat your kids will likely be different from the way they treated you, now that they have aged a little and perhaps mellowed. Regardless of how they have changed, you need to get over your grudges and your romanticism of your relationship to them for yourself and for the benefit of your children. A conversation with your parents about how you were parented is also an opportunity to inform them about how you want them to treat your children. Freedom to consciously rear your own children depends on getting over left over resentment from your own childhood. It also requires that you get over unexpressed appreciation and romanticized or idealized events.

Of the seven steps to a functional family, this first is perhaps one of the hardest because it's so easy to avoid and pretend you've done it when you haven't. But there is no way around it; you must authentically forgive your parents. Like the t-shirt my friend Grace Llewelyn gave me to wear when my twelve year old daughter watched Titanic ten times, getting over your childhood grievances is a little harsh but true. The T-shirt says, "The Ship Sank. Get Over It."

Few people make it all the way to forgiveness, because the culture we live in mitigates against it. In a big dysfunctional family where getting mad is not condoned but righteous indignation is okay, it's hard to get mad about something and get over it. To be a victim is okay. But to get pissed off and get over it and forgive and go on is taboo in polite society. That is one of the reasons the second step has to do with getting over your culture.

So let's start with that first step of getting over being victims of our parents. Then we'll see the same process is also the beginning of getting over your culture. The first step leads to the second right nicely.

I will tell you a story from my own life as an example of forgiveness.

I was ten years old. I was out behind the smokehouse, holding my screaming baby brother in my arms, hiding him from my stepfather and keeping him from watching while my stepfather beat my mother.

I couldn't keep my little one-and-a-half year old brother from hearing because I had to stay close. I couldn't run away because if I didn't stand by and listen in case I needed to run in and throw something at my stepfather, or hit him with something and run, she might die, instead of just having to go to the hospital. Sometimes I did hit my stepfather with something and then run away, to stop him from hitting or choking her. But those times when I had to leave my brother, hit my stepfather, and then run away with my stepfather chasing me. I had to escape first and then go to back to get my brother, terrified I would lead my stepfather toward us. I was also scared I might get hurt and leave my little brother screaming alone. I was desperate, terrified, furious, and also very alert—and busy making assessments about what was required next to protect my younger brothers and my mother.

Frequently, during these episodes of violence, I tried desperately to make magic, to create illusions of help from beyond for self-assurance. Inside my mind I prayed with all my might "God, please God, make him stop, please make him stop . . . " while trying to cradle and rock and walk back and forth with my brother. There were screams and thuds and sounds of things breaking. I prayed as hard as I could. After a few years of hard tries, and after being as good as I could to talk God into helping with no results, I finally concluded, when God hadn't made him stop, that God wasn't going to do anything for us. I dropped the illusion of rescue by God altogether. At the same time, I resolved, quietly, inside, that when I grew up I was going to go around killing bastards like my stepfather and rescuing poor little children like my two brothers. I would become the Lone Ranger, whose stories of dramatic justice I listened to on the radio every day. I would rescue the innocent, punish or kill the evildoers and ride off, leaving a silver bullet behind, shouting "Hi Yo Silver! Awaaayyyy!"

Once I grew a little older I had to revise that vision of heroic vengeance because I found out that the bastards like my stepfather were themselves the very helpless terrified children in need of rescue, whom I so wanted to help. Getting that insight made killing the evildoers and rescuing the children quite a bit more complicated. So, when I was sixteen years old I decided to become a psychotherapist. From that point forward I studied psychology, theology, philosophy, anthropology. I studied myself and everyone I knew. I went into individual psychotherapy, group therapy and trained as psychotherapist.

I still wanted to help people and to stop some people from hurting others so badly. I knew I was perceptive about people from the skills I had learned from trying to predict the mood and state of mind of my stepfather and of various other drunks who came to our house. I had been on guard and in training for years to protect my brothers from people whose behavior I had to accurately predict by reading their faces, gestures, speech and actions. I knew I could help people because, by the time I was in high school I had done so already, for a number of years.

I forgave my stepfather and mother before they died. I haven't completely gotten over feeling sorry for them but I am not mad at them any more. My stepfather played in a big dangerous damaging terrifying cultural game in the 1940s. The poor sonofabitch had spent six years in the Pacific in World War Two, killing people on shore from a five-inch gun aboard ship and breathing the stench of bloated floating bodies by the hundreds and sending many people to their certain death. My mother's husband dropped dead at age thirty-seven and left her with three kids, hurting and scared to death. The two of them found each other and did the best they could, which wasn't much, but I've seen worse. My lower class redneck childhood was nothing compared to your average middle class child abuse.

I got my Ph.D. when I was twenty-five years old. I still didn't know much then. I had to make a lot bigger mistakes than that. I had a lot more to learn. I had to get to know intimately many more individuals who were the destined suffering torturers of the next generation. I had to learn about how a being gets rescued from the reactive mind prison that is the source of his or her meanness. I had to get over some of my own meanness, and it took a long, long time.

I also learned that pitiful, terrified, cruel bastards like my poor stepfather, and less cruel but just mean people like myself, can't really be rescued by anyone else, they can only rescue themselves with assistance from someone else. I spent a lot of years in therapy. I hit my wives and I hit my first two children when they were adolescents. Not often, but I did it. Not anything like my stepfather, but I did shove or hit them. I also hit my brother, who is a year younger than me, a couple of times after we were grown. The buck finally stopped here, but it took a long time. I am still mean at times. I don't hit anyone anymore and haven't for a long time and don't condone it, but I think meanness is often a lot worse than hitting. I am still meaner than I want to be when I get mad, but I do that less and get over it quicker and I am grateful for that.

And finally I had to learn that even though compassion helps, a compassionate person can't make choices for other people. A compassionate person might stop someone temporarily if they are hurting a child or another person physically, or they might help provide some love for a tortured soul. They might help with a bit of a larger perspective occasionally, or some structural change in how people are treated by bureaucracies, but compassion does not include making choices for other people.

Once people are trapped in the jail of the mind, built to a great extent by how they were parented, they must free themselves. No one else can unlock the cell door but the person inside, and people who are able to free themselves not only initially, but continually, from the jail of their own minds, can be helped by friends standing by who know what the struggle is about. Those escapees are the ones who have an ongoing freedom that is characteristic of true adulthood.

I am an escapee from the mind jail and live in a community of escapees. We remind each other about what we know each time one of us re-imprisons herself. This gives us a perspective on human life and on the life of the mind that is greater than the limited cultural view into which we were born. We have all come to see that we had a tremendously advantaged childhood and we are grateful for it. The defenses we built and the images we developed of ourselves and the learning that came from having to survive various kinds of abuse, once transcended, become useful tools for creating a life.

Because of the childhood my parents and my culture afforded me, I have had a pretty clear mission all my life. I have transcended needing to help, and having transcended the need to help, I can be more helpful. I now serve people having made a decision to serve people as a free choice, rather than as a reaction to the past. I'm still neurotic. I'm still some modified kind of Lone Ranger with a savior complex. I write books and do psychotherapy and run workshops and train trainers, and consult with corporations and other organizations. Only occasionally do I threaten to beat the hell out of some bad parent on the sidewalk or in the grocery store. I haven't killed anybody for terrifying his or her children yet, though I am still secretly looking for my chance. I loved the movie Slingblade because it reminded me of my own experience with my stepfather and my own vision of vengeful justice.

Nothing in this world makes me madder than moralistic, righteous parents and teachers who take pride in multivaried forms of cruelty to their children through all the "shoulds" of socially condoned child abuse. But I have come up with a bigger vision than vengeance now, with a little help from my friends. I expect it to show up in reality by a change in how parents raise children, in the whole world, in the near future, and I want to do everything I can to help that happen before I die.

3 ⤳ FORGIVENESS

CHILDREN WHO BECOME CREATORS ARE raised by parents who have a vision of what a happy functional human being and a happy functional society look like, but who are not so attached to that vision that they ignore the current needs of the child. Getting to where you can have a vision and still pay attention to what is actually going on makes you a great parent. Parents who can do this are people who have completed their own childhoods by growing up to equality with their own parents. Forgiveness means getting mad and getting over it, getting hurt and getting over it, getting blissed out and getting over it and getting to a place where you are open to a new experience with that person, not just a rehash of an old experience.

I am harping on this so much at the beginning because a lot of people think they have forgiven their parents who haven't. You have to really forgive them in your feelings, not just in your mind, in order to be free to raise your own kids. This is a story of forgiveness of a parent, sent to us to publish in our newsletter by Liz, who was a participant in our Course in Honesty Workshop a few years back.

A STORY FROM LIZ: HOW I CAME TO RADICAL HONESTY AND GREW UP IN TWO HOURS (PLUS 48 YEARS)

It's New Year's Day, and I'm thinking about the past year and all the changes it brought. There was a move from Omaha to Kansas City and a job change, both of which were major. But without a doubt, the most significant thing that happened in 1997 is that I finally grew up by learning about Radical Honesty.

In April (I believe), with nothing better to do, I dropped by Barnes & Noble to hear some guy named Brad Blanton talk about a book that sounded interesting: Radical Honesty. The talk was free, so I thought, what the hey. As Brad talked in his inimitable way, I was amazed by his whole presentation: Physical, mental, and emotional. I'd never seen, met or even heard of anybody like this before. I imagined he was the most honest, present-in-the-moment person I'd ever seen, without the self-righteousness, airy-fairiness or solemnity of a lot of New Age fakers. He didn't proclaim that he had The Answer, freely admitted to borrowing ideas from others, yet had an air of confidence that made the humility attractive.

This Radical Honesty thing was something that was never practiced in my home when I was growing up. Everything negative was shoved under the rug, resentments were never spoken of; there was a stale, dead, toxic feel to the household that literally made me sick when I was a child. In Brad Blanton's life, I imagined, things were different, fresh, honest, free. Whatever Brad Blanton had, I wanted some of it. I didn't even stay to meet him, because I knew I would see him again. I signed the mailing list, bought the book, read it, and when I got a notice about the two-day workshop in Indianapolis in July, I went for it without hesitation.

At the two-day, the hot-seat work was intense, and I got in touch with a load of rage toward my mother. I became vulnerable, not an easy thing for me, and the support of the other people in the group was touching. I noticed that everybody became wonderful when they were vulnerable and told the truth.

As I listened to Brad's teaching sessions, I found myself making connections between many disciplines and "truths" I had learned following the New Age path. There were familiar elements, but now Brad was putting it together in a way that seemed practical and actually useful. Brad was teaching me how the mind works (like a bullshit-making machine, or a meaning-making machine) and how to free myself from the prison of my own mind. That had been the missing piece I'd been searching for nearly twenty years on a spiritual path.

By the end of the two-day, I knew I had to do my completion with my mother. I was filled with dread at the thought of it, but I knew I couldn't not do it: I was a pressure cooker filled with boiling, toxic rage, and I was close to blowing up. The anger was poisoning my relationships with everybody in my life, including myself. It was adversely affecting the job I was doing at work. The completion had to be faced—later. Maybe after the eight-day in September.

If I wondered beforehand if the eight-day Course in Honesty workshop would be worth the money and time, when it ended, I knew that what I had gained there was beyond price; namely, a chance to be real, tell my story and get over it and on to the life I wanted. When I got home and looked at my life story on videotape (after being afraid to for two weeks), I was grief-stricken. This is how I am? I don't like her. I don't want to be her. It was clear that I had been living according to my mind's distorted "story" about how things were, a story filtered through rage. I saw my whole life as a tragedy of "what might have been, if only." I needed to get over this victim story and literally get real. It was time to do the completion with my mother.

How simple it all seems now, but how difficult it seemed before doing it. On the three-hour drive to my mother's house, I felt alternate waves of despair and excitement. Every time I feared doing the completion work "wrong," I remembered Brad's advice to "do it all wrong, do a third-rate job, and fuck it all up." Most of my life, I've been immobilized by perfectionism, so this idea of intentionally doing something badly (if that's how I had to do it to get it done) was a new wrinkle. Risking looking crazy, looking ugly, being judged, causing my mother a heart attack, etc., etc., were some of the fears I had to fight down. As I drew closer to Jeff City, I felt the way I felt when I was coming down with the Hong Kong flu but didn't realize it yet: I knew something was about to happen, and I wasn't sure exactly what it was, but I suspected it would be something pretty serious and bad.

When I arrived, grim and tense, I explained to my mother what I was going to do, why I needed to do it, and how. I requested that she sit at the kitchen table and listen to me speak my resentments and appreciations to her. I requested that she not interrupt, and I told her that I would listen to what she had to say afterward. She agreed.

For the next two hours, I talked, yelled, screamed, stood up, sat down, paced around, cried, pounded on the table for emphasis, said "fuck," "shit," "damn," "God-damn," and "hell." Numerous times. This to a little old lady Christian Scientist. I told her I had sex with men I wasn't married to, and that I enjoyed it and saw nothing wrong with it. I told her I did drugs. I told her every stupid resentment I could think of—forty-eight years of resentment spewed out in two hours.

Then it was my mother's turn to talk. During my rant, she had mostly listened, but occasionally her jaw dropped, and she said, "Whaaat??" or "I don't remember that." It became clear that my remembrance of my childhood and hers were radically different. For instance, she was resentful over my not having involved her in preparations for my first wedding. She said I was very snotty to her. I didn't remember that, but allowed that it probably was because I didn't like her. There was silence for a moment, then she said quietly, "I didn't like my mother, either." I was stunned. My mother had never revealed herself like that to me before. I felt something open up inside me. I wouldn't call it love, exactly, but it was a flow of energy toward my mother.

At one point, my mother started crying, and she talked about how she wasn't going to live much longer, and now, in light of what I had said, she thought she should change her will and take my name off her house and her stock accounts. She said when she died, she didn't want a notice in the paper or a funeral, just a cremation, and that she didn't want anybody to know, and she didn't want anybody to tell me, because nobody cared. I told her I resented her for saying those things at that moment, and that I imagined she was trying to manipulate me. She knocked it off, and we went on to talk more calmly.

All in all, I give myself a C+ rating for how I did the completion (Hooray for average!), and I give my mother an A-. She was willing to withstand the toxic rage assault, and before I left, we cried together, hugged and kissed. And this time, I really wanted to hug her. I had revealed myself to her, and to the extent she could, she had revealed herself to me. I felt as if we were no longer in some set mother-daughter act, but had transcended that and were now two human beings, just being with each other. Amazingly, I felt as if I'd grown from a splintered, self-centered, petulant child into a whole, caring adult in two hours.

On the road back home, I felt as if a fresh breeze was blowing through my mind and body. It was a brilliant, sunny day. The sky was a deep autumn blue that was perfectly clear and seemed filled with unlimited potential. I felt energized, excited, light and restless. I really could have used a good reggae band to dance my brains out to. Since finding one along I-70 seemed a remote possibility, I wondered what else I could do to satisfy this tingling, excited, vital urge to do something. First, I stopped at a C-store and got a package of Hostess Snowballs and a Diet Dr Pepper. In the car, I wolfed down one of the Snowballs and slugged down some Diet Dr. Pepper, but as I kept on driving, I thought, "Well, that wasn't it. What else? What else? What do I need?"

Then I found myself making some strange sound I'd never made before. It was somewhere between singing and yelling. It was a pure, focused sound that created overtones, as in Tibetan throat-singing. That was really fun. I enjoyed the sounds for a while, then thought, "That wasn't it, either. What do I need?" Then it came to me: a Swisher Sweet. I wanted to smoke a Swisher Sweet. Where that idea came from, I don't know. I'd never smoked one in my life. My first ex used to smoke them. So I stopped at a C-store and bought some. On the way back out to the car, I fumbled with the cellophane. Adrenaline was rushing, and I broke the first one trying to get it out of the box. The second one came out okay, and I lit it, rolled down the window, drew in a mouthful of warm, pungent smoke, blew it out and sighed, "Aaaaaah!" That was it. I drove down I-70 with the plastic tip of the Swisher Sweet clamped between my teeth, feeling like FDR. As the smoke billowed out the window, I felt a profound feeling of peace, joy and well-being.

In the following week, I did completions with Winston, the guy I'd been involved with in Iowa City, and with my friend, Lynn. After each one, I felt another layer of bullshit and mind-weight had been lifted. I felt cleaner, stronger, more okay about myself.

The healing of my relationship with my mother is still evolving. When I left after our completion, I didn't know how I felt about her. I had no idea what came next, now that the Big Event was over. When I saw her at Thanksgiving, I noticed I was being more solicitous and protective toward her. I felt affectionate toward her. Then at Christmas, I was practically overwhelmed with feelings for her. Lately, I have been feeling a love for her that is so deep it hurts. I believe I am grieving. I have regrets that I didn't clear with her years ago, before she began to deteriorate physically. We might have enjoyed trips together, or just simply being together much more. Even though I have regrets, I also have gratitude that even though it took a long time, eventually I got my mother back. She didn't change; I did.

Before, looking at my childhood through a glass darkly, as it were, painting everything black and bad, I couldn't see the good. Now that the resentment has been released, I can see the good. Now I feel grateful to have had the parents I had. I remember the way I thought of the past, but now I'm not attached to it. I see quite clearly that it was a story, not reality. The facts I remembered were accurate in most cases, but because I was stuck in a negative paradigm, I omitted any facts that contradicted the story that I had a lousy, lonely childhood.

The fact is that I had two parents who loved me imperfectly. So did everybody. They did some things very well, others not so well. I've gotten off of that "they should have known better" judgment. Now I think they did pretty well, all things considered. I always had clean clothes, enough food, a nice house in a safe neighborhood, a mother who was there when I got home from school, and nobody got hit or screamed at or hauled off to jail. My parents encouraged me to learn, to be curious, to think. They gave me riding lessons, ballet and tap, piano lessons, art classes, etc., etc. They took me to museums and music concerts, and we went on vacations. My mother read to me, my dad used to make up stories about a mouse family and draw pictures of the mice that made me laugh. When my dad went on business trips, he would bring me dresses from Saks Fifth Avenue or Stix Baer & Fuller or a nice store wherever he went. And I think all of that is pretty Goddamned wonderful.

The year 1997 has been the most significant in my life, in that it was the year I finally reached adulthood in just two hours plus forty-eight years, by practicing Radical Honesty. I reclaimed my love for my mother, thereby reclaiming my ability to love others and myself. That's the most important and glorious Christmas gift I can imagine.

I still have a couple of completions to do, and I'm just as frightened about doing them as I was about doing the first one. In 1998, I am working on getting better at staying current and living out loud, figuring out how to use Radical Honesty at work, and writing up projects and finding committed listeners to help me get them done.

Thank you to Brad, Amy, Carsie and Elijah, and all of you. I appreciate you for having taught me, supported me, hugged me, listened to me, resented and appreciated me. I feel in my heart that 1998 will be an incredible year of growth—not the horrible, painful kind, but the positive, exciting kind—for all of us.

I love you all.

Liz

I continue to be in touch with Liz since she wrote this letter in 1998. Her life has been much freer, with new relationships formed, and old relationships renewed. She also changed her place of work and her participation in political efforts. She has been critical to the success of a campaign to prevent anti-evolution groups from taking over the public school curriculum.

She fell in love with a man she still cares about. She and her mother became steadily closer, and are contemplating moving into the same house together. She keeps telling the truth and her life keeps being renewed because of it. She is again in contact with her son, sharing honestly in a renewed relationship with him. She raised him before her liberation from her anger towards her mother, and he had a pretty rough life. But he has found it possible to forgive her as well.

As I said at the beginning of this chapter, forgiveness means getting mad and getting over it, getting hurt and getting over it, getting blissed out and getting over it and getting to a place where you are open to a new experience with that person, not just a rehash of an old experience. *You know when you have done it because you now like being around the person.* You don't dread seeing them anymore. Contact with them is no longer an unwanted obligation. If you don't feel that way about your parents, take care of it. The power you have to love and nourish your children depends on you having the courage to do what it takes to forgive your own parents.

4 ✑ COMPLETING YOUR OWN CHILDHOOD FOR THE SAKE OF YOUR OWN CHILDREN

IF YOU WANT TO HAVE the possibility of creating love through honest sharing and communication as a context for raising your children you have to settle things with your own source family like Liz did. What it takes to be a good parent is the same thing it takes to live the good life. Each person who becomes an adult must do some version of what Liz did, in order to own his or her own authority enough to be a parent.

Adults who are free to choose how to create their lives, because they are not hiding from anyone anymore, have the possibility of enjoying the rearing of thier own children. To feel free to create your life and to see the job that way is quite a psychological accomplishment. To do this requires taking on the authority over your own life that, more than likely, the institutions you were raised in, and your parents, trained you how *not* to do. They probably, in many ways, still have you buffaloed.

What is different about adults who have forgiven their own parents?

Parents are able to act according to their vision of the future, and pay attention to their children's current needs, only when their vision has replaced the neurotic survival mechanisms of their own psyches based on their own childhood. This means, if you want to be a good parent you have to tell your own parents the truth about who you are and what you have done and deal with the fall-out all the way through to forgiveness, pretty much like Liz described. If you can forgive your parents for all you have against them and appreciate them for all they did for you, eventually growing beyond being bound by unexpressed resentment as well as unexpressed appreciation, you can do a powerful job of parenting your own children. If can't, it is a matter of children raising children, once again.

When we are no longer simply reacting to the past with bitterness or phony "positive" attitudes, or any of the other countless lying adaptive roles we freeze into to avoid telling the truth to our former caretakers about our hurt and fury, then and only then can we envision a future for each child we are responsible for. We can see a picture in our imaginations of our child as a happy flexible creative nurturant being who continues to grow beyond belief in a world that has grown beyond belief. That picture is actually easy to live into, once pictured.

But there is more completion beyond your parents. It is hard to keep a picture of a world of freedom and experimentation worrying about the bills and the taxi service and the Joneses and the surrounding belief systems in the world of real life parenting, but it is possible—particularly if you have friends who are trying to do the same and who share the struggle with you. Friends helping each other stay free from their own minds and raising their children together are getting the help they need from each other, rather than from experts in accepted cultural ignorance.

It is important that you have an honest ongoing conversation with your own parents as an adult no longer intimidated by them enough to lie to them anymore. Children who remain children after thirty don't make good parents. A number of great family therapists (Minuchin, Satir, Schiff) advocate going back at least three generations to complete and get a transcendent perspective on one's family. Finally, forgiveness of your own parents by telling them the truth about everything you resent and everything you appreciate face to face is important preparation for parenting and grandparenting together.

The chapter entitled "Radical Honesty about Anger" in *Practicing Radical Honesty* is one of the best things I have ever written and one of the best things I have ever read about how to forgive. The Radical Parenting Workshops conducted by the Centers for Radical Honesty are organized around the principle and the process of forgiveness in order to move on in life, reparenting your own self and parenting your children out of choice rather than reaction.

CREATING A VIDEO ARCHIVE OF YOUR FAMILY

The possibility of creating video family archives for families grew out of our experience with the Eight Day Radical Honesty Workshop, which we have conducted since 1989. In these workshops sixteen people come and live with us at Sparrowhawk Farm in the Shenandoah Valley for eight days and nights. At the beginning of the workshop we all make agreements to tell the truth for the duration of the workshop. In the context of living and working together for eight days, doing Yoga for forty five minutes a day, meditating for twenty minutes twice a day, doing lots of group process work, paired exercises, lectures, videos, a selection of feature length films, running two miles a day and living in the conversation about what life is all about, one of the exercises everyone does is tell the entire story of their life, answering all questions that arise from the telling, honestly. The life stories are videotaped. The video of each person's life story is given to them, and at the end of the eight days, in preparation for the first follow up group which meets several months later, they are asked to show the video to their parents and loved ones and have a conversation with them about it. Some of these conversations are hard to face, and initiating them is hard to do and takes some courage and intentionality. Always, a modification of the worldview of the participant and usually that of their whole family occurs. This modification is almost always in the direction of forgiveness. Sometimes it takes more than one conversation after watching the video. Sometimes some of the processing is helped by having someone serving as a mediator present to facilitate the process of telling the truth about feelings. Out of this process, forgiveness occurs. The same thing usually happens in the source family that happened in the new family of the group—everyone falls in love with each other again.

The life story segment of the Radical Honesty Workshops has now grown in many instances to the development of life story archives for some families, where they begin a true family history. Everyone in the family tells the story of their life. You can do it in an hour for each person. Then you keep the videos for anyone in the family to watch whenever they like. Home video cameras have created the possibility of a deeper understanding of how families pass on their traditions and their blessings and their neuroses.

Mostly there is a lot of laughter when forgiveness shows up. I recommend that you do this with your family. It is a good way to start the process of forgiveness you need to have the freedom to actually raise your own child by choice rather than reaction. It will also help the grandparents and you to handle the job together. Whether you ever get to do these workshops or not, you can instigate a family archives conversation in your own family whenever you like.

THANKS, BUT NO THANKS

You may, like me, appreciate the culture we were raised in for all the opportunities to learn and the material well being we have experienced. Being born here was like winning the lottery. We were lucky to be advantaged and disadvantaged in this way. At the same time, you may also, like me, resent the culture we were raised in for all its moralism and outmoded institutionalized ignorance.

Really good parenting, the kind that allows children to grow up into freedom rather than jail, requires digesting our culture. We have to chew it up and spit out and otherwise eliminate what is no good for us and our children, and absorb and grow on what is nurturing and healthy, and pass that on. Our babies model for us the most needed action concerning our cultural heritage—when they indulge the way they do in the unabashed pleasure of taking a totally absorbing ecstatically pleasing bowel movement. The first step of good parenting has to do with taking a good dump frequently and enjoying the hell out of it. This way we get to grow up ourselves, and then contribute to the ongoing growth of our culture.

THE HUMAN RESEARCH PROJECT

We advocate this radical sharing of how life is for you, in depth, including all your actions, judgments and feelings, because of our view of what the opportunity of being a human being is. We think that we are all engaged in a big research project together, which involves both discovering and inventing what it is to be human. Sharing what life is actually like for you with your source family and the family that proceeds from you is a contribution of information to our developing understanding and designing of ourselves. We are the only species that gets to consciously participate in our own design. When we withhold information we don't contribute to the process of discovery and invention, we inhibit that process. We have already collected enough information about withholding. What we all need to learn more about is sharing.

Participating in this great conversation of design and discovery is one of the best games in town. It is the most intimate conversation possible. It is the fundamental act of creation in which people who love each other can participate. It is the source of family.

When you do what you need to do to tell the truth about your actions, your feelings and your opinions to those you love and fear, you have grown up to the stage of possible responsible parenthood. When you haven't, that fear that keeps you from living out loud only contributes to a continuation of the darkness, for your children as well as ours. I encourage you to do whatever it takes. Courage is only needed when there is risk. Courage is not necessary unless you are afraid. Courage is not being unafraid, it is being afraid and doing it anyway. Courage is going ahead and doing what you are afraid to do. Telling the truth to your own parents about things you've always hidden from them and are afraid to to tell them, is an act of love for your own child.

Step 11

Forgiving Your Culture

5 ✍ GOOD NEWS AND BAD NEWS

NOTHING IS MORE BEAUTIFUL THAN the innocent new being that lives and notices the world right after being born, before the mind is built. That being, who notices, continues to live behind the mind, and in spite of it. As that little being grows older and grows a mind and learns how to fit into her family and culture, she usually gets damaged or crippled by the way she is treated by her parents and teachers. This is the way things are. This is the bad news. Most of us learn unnecessary suffering and hold on to it for the rest of our lives. It seems to come with the territory of being dependent on the big people for so long before we get to take care of ourselves on our own.

It may be that the primary value of your life and mine is to serve as a warning to others. That is a rather cynical way to begin talking about our personal cultural heritage and at the same time it may be the best start we could make. I am cynical and hopeful at the same time. Getting over some of the cultural brainwashing and conventional ignorance of parents and educators from the dark ages of the Twentieth Century has been a long time coming.

It is to those untold innocent beings who have been murdered by the minds of their cultures that this book is dedicated. It is also dedicated to the possibility of an end to that ignorant cultural brainwashing we kill children with in the name of love every day. Whether it gets called education or parenting or "inculcating moral values" or "religious instruction" or whatever bullshit label gets put on it, it is fundamentally child murder.

You and I are programmed to constrain our children in the name of love and to teach them how to put a damper on their lives and be anxious and depressed and unhappy and dissatisfied with life. We are experts in how to kill their spirit a little bit at a time. We have been taught to teach our children to look for deliverance from the exigencies of living through figuring things out. We believe, in our bones, from the way we were raised, that thinking will rescue us and figuring things out will make us happy. We transmit without conscious awareness that the right way to live is to be searching for happiness and a cure for what ails us. We have been raised to believe that the key to our happiness is finding the right kinds of people to be with, the right kinds of external forms of entertainment and the right kinds of internal biochemical relief.

There are lots of experts around to make sure we do the job of teaching children how to live right according to implicit cultural biases, and to make sure we do a good job of it. I am not one of them. I can only report this with some certainty: Children are almost always more capable of being happy to begin with than they are when their parents are through with them.

Okay, then, what's the good news? The good news is that if we really get conscious of the bad news and notice how we bring it about we can change it. The good news is that we can overthrow the government. We can overthrow the government of the mind. "I think, therefore I am," was a mistake. After thousands of useless wars and hundreds of thousands of wasted lives and unnecessary suffering and death we can now know this. "I am, therefore I think," is a better formulation to live by. It is also a better formulation to raise our children by.

Okay, back to the bad news. Just remember this: Since getting the bad news is critical to getting the good news, getting the bad news is good. Being a good parent absolutely requires a comprehensive view of the bad news. So let's look more thoroughly at the bad news.

WHAT MAKES PEOPLE UNHAPPY AND UNFREE?

In our culture, in the western world (which is the model now being copied by the rest of the world), we have come to value money and the material comforts it provides more than being with children. We're abandoning our children when they are very young and leaving them to caretakers other than ourselves, using the rationalization that we have to do that in order to take care of our children. This is a terrible mistake.

These caretakers do the best they can, but for the most part do not love the child like a parent who bonds with their own child upon its arrival. (Although a lot of parents miss the best opportunity to bond with their children anyway, by giving birth in hospitals, where almost everything that can be done to block bonding occurs.) Usually, in spite of this missed opportunity at the very beginning, parents still love their children and do the best they can, based on what they know, to take care of them. The problem is that the best way they know is, in many ways, insane. The culture we live in, the one that is taking over the world, is insane.

Cultures, like people, are not just crazy and that's all there is to it. There is more to them than just their insanity. A lot of crazy people have many charming and useful characteristics other than the fact that they are crazy. A lot about our culture is fine too, but like a photocopy machine with no power to choose, when we carry on the culture the bad gets copied along with the good. Errors are maintained and don't get corrected. We, in the West, have material well being and access to information and entertainment and good roads and food and shelter for the most part and extensive fine communication networks and many other wonderful opportunities—and they are all tied in somehow with our generally unhappy citizens.

Though there are some class differences in how our children are raised, rich or poor, the way we raise our children in this culture is not one of our strengths. We can tell this by talking to so-called grownups. You know a lot of people. What do you think? Aren't most of the adults you know generally screwed up? Aren't most of your friends less than happy, not living up to their full potential, lying and sneaking around a lot, getting by with what they can and generally, furtively, looking here and there for a little relief or pleasure or freedom? Don't they waste a lot of energy more or less desperately pretending that everything is all right? Don't you? By the time most of us grow up, we are not dealing with a full deck, not happy, not firing on all cylinders and can't find our way around in life and relationships worth a damn. Don't you want your children to be happier than most of the people you know are? Including yourself?

We have all gone crazy together. We are crazy over money. The whole world is involved. The best and most nurturing cultures are succumbing to the influence of multi-national corporations for the sake of toys advertised on TV. The average workweek in 1954 was seventeen (17!) hours shorter than in 1994. In forty years of the greatest technological advances in history, with more labor saving devices than any humans in history could have ever imagined, the workweek for all of us got seventeen hours longer! Not only that, if you take into account the real value of the money made in terms of purchasing power, the current captains of industry have two workers for the same price they paid for one in 1954!

It's a great thing that women can work and compete in the marketplace but it is incredibly stupid for men and women to have children together and both keep working fifty-five to sixty hours a week. This is particularly true when the children are young. It is completely ass backwards for parents to be working all the time to care for children they are not actually, in reality, caring for. Single parents have even fewer options. The story just gets worse.

It is time for a revolution. If you are a parent the revolution is up to you. I don't mean a phony Republican revolution with welfare reform that impoverishes another million and a half children to protect the poor helpless rich people. I don't mean a phony Democratic revolution where the drop in the bucket of having paid leave for parents when children are sick is hailed as a great leap forward. I mean a revolution, a turning of the wheel, that comes from waking up and seeing the stupidity of what we have all been doing, and giving it up.

Listen. Grab your children and run. Head for the nearest exit. Regardless of your circumstances, if you leave your child with others more than six hours a day, five days a week, I don't care how you do it just quit doing that right now. Don't feel guilty and do nothing about it and try to compensate with so called "quality time" and screw your child up further, either. Regardless of what other people tell you, you are making a mistake when you do that.

We're making a terrible mistake. Just because we are all making the same mistake together doesn't make it less of a mistake. These little damaged souls whose parents deprived themselves and their offspring of common nurturance, and violated 50,000 years of genetic programming about how to birth and raise children, these hurt children will themselves parent the next generation with God knows what distorted capacity to love—in fact they already are.

Many of these hurt children raising children don't read. But you do. Please use what you read here to further the revolution of the hurt children to save the future children by raising your child in a more intelligent way than you were raised. Let me know. You can be in the movie we make about this book, and the sequel to this book, Practicing Radical Parenting: Stories of Successful Families Whose Kids Turned Out Happy.

MORE GOOD NEWS—
WE ARE ALL NATURALLY INCLINED TO BE GOOD PARENTS

Children are still the most fun, significant, meaningful, fulfilling wonderful opportunity to be alive and in love that exists on the face of the planet. We are built that way. It's a part of our genetic design as a species. We have to take a long time to get our children on their feet because we are built that way. They need us and we need them. That long time is what allows us to bond with and be bonded with children, and so grow a mind and heart that are informed with the very practical experience of love. We are programmed with a simple instinctual common sense function of noticing what is needed to take care of ourselves and our own, and then simply doing what we've noticed is needed, but many people in our culture have lost touch with this natural ability.

HOW OUR MINDS CAPTURE THE SPACE OF FREEDOM

For minds that have bought the principle that the purpose of life is to make a living, no further contact with reality is necessary. These minds have organized themselves into a collective insanity with a mission. Their mission is to recruit children into the marketplace via the school system with the help of lawyers on boards of directors who are trained experts in insanity. It's no wonder there are so many la la land freak religions and teachers and self help moon beam idiots on every block with delusional charlatan emotional cripples moralizing to other adult aged children even more lost than themselves. There are a lot of ignorant and insane and bad people who are after you and your children out there.

Your children are needed for the market, the defense industry, the military and the other antiquated institutions of our culture. I am not talking about the ghetto, where your child can be killed by a bullet just for being there. I am talking about the ghetto of the school system, teacher training, parenting, television—the entire culture—upper, lower and middle class in which we live. You can't go wrong by being totally paranoid about this. Middle-class child abuse is probably worse than lower class child abuse.

The lost children I've seen as clients in my psychotherapy practice in Washington, D.C. for the last twenty-five years make anywhere from zero to a half million dollars a year and spend a lot of it on bogus books and tapes. The publishing industry pours out pre-life past-life pro-life post-life lame-brained so-called self-help bullshit by the ton. The producers of this bullshit are generally in worse shape than the consumers. Any delusional belief system other than reality will do. The dumbbells who write those books are all in an unconscious conspiracy with NASDAQ too. How in the hell else could politicians and lawyers run the world and keep the other emotional cripples out of their way and off welfare and unaware of the corporate welfare program called the defense industry? From fall out shelters to the war on drugs the path of corporate government is strewn with the litter of ignorance and waste. Let's not raise our children to fit into this overwhelmingly stupid arrangement.

We have all been trained to think if you're rich you must be smart and vice versa. I'll be goddamned if that's so. There are rich people by the ton out there trying to win the Darwin award every day. (The Darwin award is given to people who die at their own hands through ingenious innovation that turned out to be fatal ignorance. They are given the award in gratitude for having had the grace to remove themselves from the gene pool.) Having a mind at all is a mixed blessing but having a mind filled with the cultural preconceptions of modern times is dangerous to your health and well-being and dangerous to the health and well being of others. Any competent mental health professional, upon reviewing the possibility of damage to self or others, would commit this culture to the mental hospital for its own protection immediately.

It is because we have minds that you cannot plumb the depths of human ignorance. You also cannot charge too much for it. The farther out the delusion, the more "new age" it is, the more you can charge for it. Particularly is this true with so-called PSYKO therapy. Our age of pop-psych so-called sophistication reminds me of the earlier part of the Twentieth Century when a mystical belief in science first became a fad for the masses. A good shuck at that time was to go around "re-charging" people's lightning rods on their houses and barns by hooking up a battery from a car to the lightning rods for a couple of hours. "Keeps your house from being struck by lightning" was sold for anywhere from a buck to five dollars by traveling hucksters for decades. Most psychotherapists and most new age self help gurus are running a similar shuck. For a little more money they will recharge your personal lightning rods so you won't get struck by lightning, or have to take responsibility for yourself as an adult.

I know I rant and go on and on. But listen, this is important: A parenting and education system now exists almost world-wide that systematically blinds people to basic discriminations necessary for taking care of themselves, and makes them amenable to sales pitches from every quarter. The way the world economy is set up we need a high proportion of emotional cripples to keep the economy going. Religion is in a conspiracy with the Dow Jones Industrial Average to keep us in slavery.

You and I are the secret agents of this system, even when we don't agree with it. We have to get on to ourselves and heal ourselves somewhat of our brainwashing in order to do a halfway competent job of raising our kids. We have to learn how we use beliefs to block noticing, and then help each other get over it before we pass this virus on to our children. We have to learn how beliefs are the source of the unbelievable ignorance that makes horrific lower, middle and upper class child abuse commonplace.

6 ✍ THE EVOLUTION OF PARENTING IN MODERN TIMES

HOW TO RAISE CHILDREN HAS been an important conversation to human beings since human beings started having conversations. In order to catch up on this conversation, let's start out here with a short overview of the recent history of child-rearing in America.

In Twentieth Century America, childhood became increasingly institutionalized in response to industrialization. Schools designed on the industrial model, reflecting the ideals of standardization, production, efficiency, and division of labor, were developed. They dominate children's lives, with the purpose of preparing them to live adult lives dominated by production and consumption. Partly in response to the social upheavals of the '60s, combined with scientific developments in the theory of evolution, as well as anthropology and psychology, childhood at the beginning of the Twenty-first Century is being reinvented. The difference has to do with children being viewed as being all right the way they are—trusting the natural process of growth, maturation, and development. This is radically new when measured against history: the ideas of original sin, of beating decency into the heathen, of the flesh being base and sinful. Dr. Spock's common-sense approach has been gradually replacing tight-fisted moralism.

The modern movement to recapture the natural order of infancy and growth from pseudo-scientific technological interference began during the 1950s. In 1956 the La Leche League was formed by mothers to support and endorse breastfeeding and natural childbirth. Today, magazines such as "Mothering" promote extended breastfeeding, natural childbirth, the family bed, natural health, "continuum parenting," and home schooling. This and many other magazines and advocacy groups connect together a loose network of parents, midwives, healers, and educators to develop and explore the possibilities of a peaceful, loving childhood lived in the family rather than in institutions. What makes these people radical is that they are reactionary. They envision getting back to basics in quite a serious sense.

The home schooling movement, erroneously understood by some to be an eccentricity of the Christian right, is actually a reflection of the large numbers of parents who have for various reasons discovered that children do better, learn more, are happier and healthier and better socialized, when their lives are lived in the real world, surrounded by their families. They've learned that education as preparation for life is an unnecessary concept. They assume that education and living are an integrated, ongoing, and lifelong experience. They no longer assume, nor do their children assume, that someday their education will be over and life will begin. Both the fundamentalist Christians who fear the "secular humanist" philosophy supposedly promoted in public schools, and the left-wing "unschoolers" who keep their children home for academic and philosophical reasons, have discovered the advantages of the non-institutional life. This has all gone on at the same time as the increased institutionalization of children—

more school, earlier school, longer hours at school, year-round school and day care at school. Some states attach continued receipt by parents of welfare checks and food stamps to their children continuing in school. People who stay in school are more manageable, the philosophy goes.

However, if John Naisbitt and Patricia Aburdene's predictions in *Megatrends 2000* (Avon, 1999) concerning work in the information age are true, twenty-five years or less from now, 40% of all workers will work mostly from home. Today's high school graduate can expect to have five entirely different careers by the time she reaches retirement. An institutional preparation for an institutionalized life is clearly already an anachronism. The new trend where parents take primary responsibility for the care and rearing of infants in a community or tribal context, extending to the education of children in later childhood, is creating a new form of parenting, much like the very ancient form. The title of Hillary Clinton's recent book on child-rearing, *It Takes a Village* (Touchstone, 1996), as well as much of the content, makes this point quite well.

Some things about how we raise and educate our children no longer fit what is needed for human beings to participate in the likely society of the future. There is no need for grouping children in peer age groups to teach age-appropriate lessons. We know we can trace individual rates and patterns of growth more accurately than that. There is no need for ratios of more than three or four children per adult, rather than the ridiculous thirty-to-one ratio of many classrooms. There is no need whatsoever anymore for school buildings with classrooms that hold thirty children of the same age group. This list can go on and on. But if we cut to the chase it is clear that there is no need for schools as we have known them at all anymore. There is no need for teachers as we have known them. There is no need for teacher training as we have known it.

There is a need for raising children who will, as adults, very likely be based at home, communicate a lot with other people using electronic devices, do work that is probably not geographically constrained, be able to learn new information as it emerges, and consider work a chance to play and serve other people.

We are at a crossroads in this conversation about education and child-rearing today. Our educational institutions are a failure by their own standards, much less by standards that transcend the limitations of intellectual learning alone. We are building more prisons, reforming welfare, engaging in perennially boring and ignorant political debate, and inding scapegoats to blame for society going to hell in a handbasket. Superficial solutions to reductionistically isolated problems are proposed every day by lobbyists with law school training who instruct legislators at the behest of corporations. They even write up draft legislation and accompanying regulations "just to help."

If we fool citizens can be buffaloed by having our ire raised with stories of how we are being ripped off by welfare recipients with ungrateful attitudes who are "abusing" the system and wasting millions, maybe we can be distracted from noticing the way we are being ripped off for billions every month by corporations who are our "friends." Labor saving devices surround us to such an extent we don't have time for anything anymore. We rush through our lives trying to make ends meet, trying to make deadlines. What we all need are lifelines, not deadlines. We weren't built to live this way.

There are many ways of taking care of little ones until they grow up which have become tradition in our parenting and educational culture. These ways didn't ever really work well, even when there was a perceived primary need for factory workers and soldiers. They resulted in classrooms for thirty or more students, sitting in desks in rows, taught with moral rigidity on the part of teachers, with excessive emphasis on politeness and behaving, coming and going promptly with the ringing of bells. These ways never worked well to make human beings happy in the past. They are even less applicable to our likely future. Valuing order more than learning as a primary educational value is even more inappropriate for our likely future than it was for our unhappy recent past. We weren't built to live that way, and no amount of persistent force in the wrong direction will change that.

STEP III

GAINING A NEW PERSPECTIVE
ON BEING A HUMAN BEING
THAT TRANSCENDS YOUR CULTURE

7 ✑ TRANSCENDING AMERICAN CULTURAL VALUES—THE CURRENT STANDARD FOR THE WORLD

ONE OF THE SACRED, A PRIORI assumptions of current conservative political philosophy is that the reason the culture is going to hell is that there is not enough—or good enough—training in moral values at an early age. The theory goes that if them coloreds and white trash would just train their children better the world would be a better place. Their children may come up miserable but at least be well behaved in their misery like the privileged classes, and the privileged can at least keep the money. Since these pitiful middle and upper class cripples breed and proceed as they do, the only hope for the survival of the world must come from us coloreds and white trash and wimmen and other second class citizens.

So I'm writing this book. I'm white trash with a Ph.D. Carsie, our daughter, who is also helping with this book, is just fourteen and ain't gone to school a lick in her life until year before last, when she was attending as a spy. And Elijah, who is only seven, is a main source of a lot of what is said here. He is one of many seven-year-olds who make up the real threat to the current world standard belief system.

THE TRUTH ABOUT ALL CULTURES

Cultures operate consistent with a mythology that allows them to focus the energy of their members toward certain ends. This is so conditions and institutions can be created to benefit the people of the culture. The cost of this focus is that it limits what we can notice outside the mindset of the myths we live by. Our culture has, as cultures will, taught its members to be ignorant.

I imagine you are engaged in the middle of life with other people, including children, doing your best to responsibly care for your children and raise them right. I'm sure you're well intentioned. But well intentioned people screw up their children every damned day because of highly valued and unquestioned cultural ignorance, moralism, righteousness, paranoia, obsessiveness and other charming human characteristics. I'm sure you, like me, have plenty of them. We all have minds within which our culture lives—minds full of hopelessly obsolete subsets of ignorant prejudice which compete with each other for dominance. I know this from personal experience with lots of parents. I also have plenty of bullshit of my own and produce my fair share every day. This is where I'm starting from, in my assumptions about you and your mind.

I love being and I love beings. I have very little respect for minds. I imagine you are an ignorant person, well intentioned but pathetic. If that offends you it more or less proves my point. The reason I know you are living in an illusion is because we all are—all the time. Most of us don't know it, and for that reason we are living out a script written years ago that determines almost everything we do, including how we raise our children.

LET'S TAKE A BRAND NEW LOOK AT WHAT A CHILD NEEDS

What if we approached the task of parenting from a different beginning point than the moralism our culture has trained us to strive for? Just what have we learned as a benefit of our studies of ourselves in the course of the Twentieth Century?

I think the best starting point for rescuing our children from our automatic assumptions is the perspective provided by sociobiology. this is the recently emerging field which compares our new understanding of genetic programming to the archaeological, anthropological and historical record. We can now look at how we evolved and consider which genetic and behavioral adaptations helped us survive as a species, and compare that with what we know about how we lived in the world as those changes happened. This allows us a possible perspective a little different from the set of beliefs that live in our minds taught to us by our provincial culture.

We can now see the possibility of educating our children while honoring their biological genetic programming. We can also see when our biological evolution is violated. For example, the birthing of human babies that has evolved over the last 500,000 years probably shouldn't be completely rearranged and violated by some male gynecologist so he doesn't have to bend over too much when he "delivers" babies, or to suit his golfing commitments. It is clear from the work of Jared Diamond *(The Third Chimpanzee)* and the work of Jean Liedloff *(The Continuum Concept)* and the work of Thomas Lewis, Fari Amini and Richard Lannon, M.D. *(A General Theory of Love)* that birthing and rearing a child for the first year or so is critical to the remainder of the child's life for reasons Freud never even dreamed of. A new respect for where we came from in our genetic evolutionary history gives us both perspective and permission to question precious cultural assumptions we might otherwise take for granted. The practices of our culture that have been inconsistent with the last 500,000 years of genetic evolution for the birthing and early survival of children can be, and are being, changed as a result of this work.

As children continue to grow beyond those first few months the story doesn't get any better. As these already-damaged little *Homo sapiens* grow older we further increase their alienation from the continuum of growth built into them over eons of time, through what we call "education." Our major recent mistake has been that we have been too focused on agendas for the future that are intended to prepare children for intellectual communication so they can successfully participate in the economy and society as adults. We start too early and work too hard at it. This doesn't help them, it hurts them. Exactly how we hurt them by trying to help them is becoming clearer.

Economic privilege is a form of moralism that substitutes money for other values. Competition for economic privilege is all the rage now, and the source of more rage than most people can imagine. The agenda of economic success through academic success, which is our favorite commonly agreed-upon form of insanity in current world culture, is based on an antiquated industrial model. It is long dead, but our institutions can't keep up. Even the most snobbish of these institutions have been dead for a long time but just haven't fallen down yet, because blind faith in ignorant belief sustains them. They keep their eyes on the prize way after the prize isn't there anymore.

While we ourselves are focused on an agenda of conceptual learning alone, we fail to notice the baby, overlooking the importance of touch and smell and sound at an early age. We start out with our little babies by living in our heads and ignoring their needs, while the baby learns that the world is a place of deprivation and torture.

But there are some new ideas afoot. They are based on discovering, through group psychotherapy and personal growth and addiction recovery groups, how to get over some of the damage done. They follow this line of reasoning: Because most of us have been tortured by resentful, well-meaning folk trying to teach us something for our own good, and have become unconscious of our resentment for being treated that way, most of us are moralists. Moralists like to torture children. Since we can't shoot all the moralists without committing suicide, how about seeing what would happen if we tried educating our children from the beginning by paying attention to them rather than thinking about how they should be forced to turn out? This is a good idea.

COMMON SENSE AS AN ALTERNATIVE TO MORALISM

Moralists lack common sense. Dr. Benjamin Spock's *Baby and Child Care* (Second Edition, Pocket, 1948) which first came out before the midpoint of this most murderous of all centuries, stated eloquently a principle which is anathema to moralists: "Love and enjoy your child for what he is . . . and forget about the qualities he doesn't have. The child who is appreciated for what he is . . . will have a spirit that will make the best of all the capacities that he has and of all the opportunities that come his way." It gives me pleasure to acknowledge Benjamin Spock for the truly great man he was. Except for some rare exceptions he was a fairly sane voice in insane times. I consider *Radical Parenting* to be indebted to his legacy. In our current cultural insanity, a back-to-nature kind of common sense can help.

A Radical Parent is someone who continues to be fascinated with his child as he and they both continue to grow. "Radical" means to get to the juice in the roots of things. A Radical Parent gets to the juice in the roots of things in the here and now, which means she is more interested in what is actually going on with her child right now than with how that child is going to fit in at some future time. Fitting in is important if you are a cog. A Radical Parent is someone who sees society as a conversation that changes all the time rather than a machine to be maintained or an institution to be worshipped. A Radical Parent is someone with uncommon common sense. You may be willing to become one. You may already be one. I wish you well and I hope this helps with what you are already doing.

8 ✍ WHAT MAKES PEOPLE HAPPY AND FREE? FALLING IN LOVE, FALLING OUT OF LOVE, FALLING BACK IN LOVE

RADICAL PARENTING IS BONDING AND staying closely bonded with your child particularly in the first two years of life, and then remaining bonded with the being of your child—regardless of how many fights your minds can come up with—until one of you dies. Radical moms and dads I have known still have that ongoing intimate conversation with their children as though they were living and talking within each others' heads, no matter how old the child gets. It's as if both parent and offspring are saying at the same time, "You, I know. And you know me. I am glad we can know each other like this." It is not a power struggle, or an attempt to control or dominate or manipulate. It is not a resistance to the child growing up, or a need to always agree. It is a sharing of how each is witness to their life. It is a connection based on many memories of closely sharing, of empathy and love. It doesn't happen all the time. When it does, it's the most wonderful thing in the world for both parent and child.

BONDING

Nature provides a biochemical basis for bonding in two known instances; when post-pubescent males and females "fall in love," and when a baby is born and the parents "fall in love" with the baby. There is built-in biochemical support to get males and females together in the first place that lasts for six months to two years. There is biochemical support for re-bonding when the first baby is born and it recurs with each childbirth. After that, we're on our own. And the first year of life with the firstborn child is, for many couples, the beginning of the end of the marriage, because it tests the bond initially formed between the two parents.

The sociobiological perspective on sex has been elaborated on by Pat Love (that's really her name) who is a couples and sex therapist. In her book entitled *Hot Monogamy* she summarizes the most recent perspective on the biochemical makeup of "falling in love." In this view, falling in love occurs when there is a sudden increased flow into the bloodstream of the peptide phenylethylamine, possibly triggered by an association between some early childhood experience and some characteristic of the lover. This hormone has the effect of making the person "in love" feel full of energy, horny all the time, eat less, talk and laugh more—all the things we commonly attribute to falling in love. This peptide-based love runs out after six months to two years, which is just enough time for the human pair to meet, greet and procreate. After a maximum of two years, if a child is not born, they are on their own.

If a child does get born, both the female and the male experience temporary hormonal changes resulting in extra endorphins in their bloodstream. After that we can no longer depend on our internal biochemistry to keep us "in love" even though that was probably what got us involved in the first place.

So the question arises: What do the two of you do when you are on your own and love is just a memory? Of course, our minds, throughout history, have come up with numerous explanations about what was going on when our hormones got triggered, as minds are wont to do. We have explanations to spare about what makes our lover or our child so endearing. We do not want our explanations contradicted in these serious matters and we're ready to fight anyone who contradicts those explanations—particularly when they are saying we are just temporarily high on a very good drug that will wear off in a while and we'll just be like any other junkie left with memories but no longer capable of the high we used to get. When our highs wear off, we, as usual, come up with a plethora of explanations about who is to blame and why. We blame ourselves, our lovers, our upbringing. We work overtime with our minds "trying to understand" or "trying to figure out what is going on with us." Regardless of what theories we come up with, if we stay with the biochemical evidence, the maximum length of time we can expect internal biochemical support for a relationship, with a long peptide run and some endorphin support from making babies, is about four years. That turns out to be exactly the average length of time, worldwide, that committed monogamous relationships last. I think this is more than a coincidence. Regardless of religion, location on the planet, climate and culture, the overall average length of monogamous commitment is four years. (From The Anatomy of Love [Fawcett, 1995], by Helen Fisher.)

Furthermore, though pair-bonding for life does occur in some species, human beings do not seem to be genetically programmed for it. Even though it does occur with some regularity in human couples it is definitely not a predictable certainty in any individual case. Somewhere between 20% to 30% of all children born, worldwide, are not sired by the male in the primary paired relationship with the mother. That is, regardless of religion or religious beliefs, in whatever climate, wherever human beings are located on the planet, if you do a blood test of all the children and compare it with the blood work of the purported father, in twenty to thirty percent of the cases you won't get a match. That's why Jared Diamond calls us the species that is "70% monogamous." Most of the time these secret matings are lied about to the primary male, just as the primary male lies to his partner about his escapades.

In the United States these days we have a 53% divorce rate. I think that is not the tragedy it appears to be. The real tragedy is that in the 47% of pairs who stay together, most of those relationships are miserable, lying, depressed, bitter or poisonous to the couple and their offspring as well. Many people stay together out of fear of being alone, choosing to stay with the devil they know rather than risking a possibly greater tragedy.

I hate to be so cheerful, right at the start here but a baseline acknowledgment of what is so about human coupling is actually a better basis for deciding how to raise a child than the typical romantic idealism our culture usually provides. That idealism is doomed to disappointment. Hang in there, there's more.

For all of human history until about 300 years ago, it has taken two parents minimum, and usually a group of other adults as well, to have children be able to survive the first two years of life often enough for our species to continue. Those of us that tended to pair up and live in bunches tended to have our children survive. Those of us who didn't, died out. We are very much like the species of birds Diamond talks about, in which survival of the chicks depends on the mating pair working together to build the nest, sit on the eggs, and go for food continuously when the chicks hatch. If both members of the pair don't do their jobs the chicks won't live.

Let's say the male bird is out foraging and finds an earthworm. On the way back he spots another female of the same species. He puts down his worm, runs over and jumps her, comes back and gets his worm and takes it to feed the kids. That behavior seems kind of funny to picture and kind of familiar. Those birds are a lot like us.

So we're human. We have these reactions. Some of them are biochemical. Some of them are from our unconscious associative minds. We have always had some belief system or other to attempt to explain our reactions according to whatever cultural quagmire of explanation we got born into.

What happens to the kids in any given culture—how they get treated from birth onward—depends on which bullshit the culture uses for glue after the internal biochemical support runs out. What happens to the parent's relationship after the honeymoon is over depends somewhat on their culture as well, and on the recurrence of limbic and biochemical bonding between the two with each new child. To me it seems clear that honesty between the two about all their feelings and thoughts and reactions, sharing how life is for each of them at a deep level, is what makes for authentic success in that recurrent process of rebonding. In fact, I think this is the most important ingredient in successfully co-parenting a child.

Lots of women throughout history have just kept getting pregnant to get another hit of the internal drugs that come with making and raising babies. After all, it is better than disillusionment, depression, and facing the abyss of the meaninglessness of life. The Catholic solution for the good life is to become a biochemical and baby manufacturing plant. Though not all bad as a biochemical solution, it has some drawbacks, including the fact that this is a strategy the world can no longer afford.

A MANUAL FOR LIFE FOR THE NEWBORN

What if there was such a thing as reincarnation, and the future human, prior to conception and birth, was given a manual, just to remind her what to expect? It would read something like this: "Okay kid, here's what you're headed into. You're going to start out as a one-celled creature and build up over a long time in a place called a womb. It's warm and pleasant and nobody bothers you much. There is this dawning of experience, a noticing comes on, somewhere after about four or five months in there. It seems to get bigger slowly for just forever. After about eight to ten months things get real crowded and eventually you get too big to stay in there so you are squeezed out. It hurts some, and the place you end up getting squeezed into is not at all like where you were. You get moved around a lot, and touched a lot and fed a lot and you keep growing. It turns out there are two main people that do that stuff to you and they both often really like it and really like you at the beginning. They are called mommy and daddy. After a while, though, even though they both still love you, they start getting these bad moods every now and then. The mommy seems to have some objection to being woken up every two hours and the daddy gets pissed off and leaves a lot. He gets mad at the mommy because she gives all the attention to you that she used to give him. And he gets mad that you get her titties all the time and he doesn't anymore and he has always liked them as much as you do. He loves you and he's glad she loves you but he's just pissed off about not getting affection and sex, which you will learn more about later on in life.

"You'll learn to smile and wiggle and roll over and scootch along and crawl and walk. You'll learn to speak. As you get older you'll get to be more and more entertaining to those main two and also other people bigger than you who are around you. Then after a while they will gradually quit thinking you're so entertaining.

"They'll start feeding you bullshit at about the same time they start feeding you mashed carrots, and it will keep on like that until either they split up, or you grow up, or both, and you start the whole thing over again. If you are lucky in the beginning, one of the bigger ones will stay close to you and help out a lot by just being there. If not, you're pretty much on your own except for dumb luck. Got it? Okay, go."

9 ✒ NOTHING TO TRULY BELIEVE IN

ALL THE MAJOR SCIENTIFIC DISCOVERIES of the Twentieth Century have been based on shifts in perspective. Einstein invented the theory of relativity, tried it out in space and with subatomic particles and it worked. He looked at the world differently than had Newton, whose model also works. If you want to build a doghouse use Newton's theory. If you want to build a bomb use Einstein's (but use Newton's again to actually build it).

We have discovered that perspective is a matter of invention and that different perspectives yield different information and that all of the information is to be judged with regard to its usefulness rather that whether it is "right" or "wrong." Because of our cultural brainwashing, you and I seldom see beyond the ongoing desperate declarations and searches to discover and do what is "right" and avoid what is "wrong." We can hardly even imagine valuing several alternative approaches at one time.

In physics, psychology, linguistics, economics, sociology, theology, and philosophy—the list goes on—all the advances are in the direction of the relativity of models. Models of all kinds are subsumed under what I call the tissue box model; you use one and throw it away. When the full implications of this are finally integrated into religion, education, family life, government, organizational development, and psychotherapy, the world will be quite a different kind of place, and very suddenly.

All beliefs are relative. All models are just functional or dysfunctional towards certain ends. All models are dysfunctional when we attempt to use them where they don't serve. Nothing is sacred except that nothing is sacred. All shoulds are relative. All obligations, mindsets, ideas, gods are mere structures of belief for certain ends. All personal life stories are just stories. All concepts are fictional. All constructs are imaginary. Nothing is absolute. Possibility is not determined by belief. The greatest intellectual advance of the Twentieth Century was that through the integration of Eastern and Western thought, it is now possible to question all belief.

The transcendence of moralism, the main sickness of our time, requires detachment enough to see cultural moral values merely as beliefs. The use and abuse of belief is the fundamental issue for the Twenty-first Century.

THE INTEGRATION OF KNOWING AND BELIEVING

Western philosophy reflects a faith in thinking, while Eastern philosophy reflects a faith in noticing. The human groups of the world have slowly begun to learn from each other that both thinking and noticing are important. We have also learned, however, that thinking often blocks noticing. Nowhere is this more obvious than with regard to the limitations of cultural beliefs.

A Unitarian minister named Randle E. Vining, in a published sermon, said, "The opposite of belief is experience. If you experience something then you know it is the truth, but the same thing believed is a lie. IF YOU EXPERIENCE SOMETHING, THEN YOU KNOW IT'S THE TRUTH, BUT THE SAME THING BELIEVED IS A LIE! But, you say, we can't function without beliefs! Well, I agree that we can't function without theories and ideas. We do need a mental framework to help us interpret our experience of the world. But ideas are not like religious beliefs, because we wouldn't claim any certainty for them. They are working hypotheses—I call them notions. A belief is a hardened notion, and a believer is someone who's suffering from hardening of the notions."

What Randle Vining is talking about is the tendency we all have to categorize our experience and then, when we recall the category, we think we have recalled the experience. For example, many of us have had the peak experience of suddenly being delivered from the burden of intense worry and avoidance, and the delivery into a new experience of freedom, like that described by people who have been "saved." We then think, "that was a wonderful experience and I should never forget it and everyone should have it." This originally generous impulse quickly becomes a belief based on that memory, and a "should"—a moralistic value to be imposed on others whether they are interested or not. Then we join up together with other believers and we are off to the races. Never underestimate the power of ignorant people in large groups.

True believers of all kinds are liars (because they claim to be certain about what cannot be known) and damned dangerous. Believers are not peacemakers even if they profess a belief in peace. Believers are killers. Any of us who are still proud of forbears who fought in any war haven't yet benefited from the primary intellectual advance of the Twentieth Century. People who profess certainty about what they cannot possibly know will form up in gangs and arm themselves and kill those who don't join them in the lie they are perpetrating.

Currently there are still a lot of dangerous believers. Baptists, who propagate the shuck that there is an infallible book written by God, number about fourteen million. Catholics, who claim to be certain of an infallible man, number about 760 million. Mormons—the golden book—about four million. Muslims, with all that Shiite in them about worshipping both a man and a book—another 750 million. True Communists—hard to tell, now but there are still well over two billion candidates for true believership in *Das Kapital* and Mao's *Little Red Book* and whatever the hell is the current Nazi communist belief fashion of the decade. If we add in all the other random fundamentalists it becomes clear that of the six billion plus people in the world at the present time, the great majority are proud enough to be believers to claim membership in a believer group. This doesn't even count all the individualistic picayune small time fruitcake true believers in atheism or anarchy, or my own faith, futilitarianism, who are just as crippled in untold ways as fundamentalist religious freaks.

Most of the children born into the world have their spirits murdered by the true believers into whose hands they were born. All the blinded, deafened, desensitized, emasculated, female-circumcised, ignorant idiots who are the parents of these children are then proud the torch has been passed on. The bullshit beliefs are maintained and everyone congratulates each other on their mutual wisdom.

The world is still suffering mightily from believers. True believers value their beliefs more than they value other people. Other people are expendable as long as the beliefs can be maintained. Their own children are expendable. Examples show up in the news on a daily basis. Pakistanis and Indians, Arabs and Jews, Catholics and Protestants, Serbs and Croats, Moslems and Christians, Tutsis and Hutus, can all vouch for the ultimate importance of being right and how it justifies murder. As long as people are less important than belief the world will continue to go to hell in a handbasket. That's what I believe. How's that for a belief?

Listen. This is how our minds work. If you really want to hide something, put it behind a belief—preferably a belief about what it is you want to hide. If you want to avoid the experience of love, hide behind a belief in love. If you want protection from any uncontrollable feelings, make up some belief about them and hold on for dear death. Because, as you know, from how you were raised, when you are ensconced in belief, you're safe. You won't have to feel anything you didn't anticipate and don't already have an explanation for.

HERETICS WHO ARE BEYOND BELIEF

There is a significant and rapidly growing minority of people in the world who realize personally the relativity of belief. We have discovered and invented ways to learn detachment from belief. We have let up on our demand that belief be given the status of reality. We don't want our children raised that way anymore. If you read beyond this point you are one of us.

So far I have just been ranting on and on about the ways the world doesn't work and how dark the dark ages were up until now, and how perspective is critical to action. Now I can tell you plainly: This is a training manual about how to raise heretics. I am not alone. I am one of many, engaged in the completely futile task of trying to build a church composed entirely of heretics. It's like trying to herd cats, or load frogs in a wheelbarrow. And even though you can learn something by reading this book, I recommend that you not believe a thing I say. Use this to inform your noticing, but hold noticing as primary, and more important than ideas. If you are able to do that in regard to your children you will learn more from that than from any book on child-rearing ever written.

THE SYNTHESIS OF EAST AND WEST AND BIRTH OF WORLD-WIDE WISDOM

The overbalanced stress on thinking by Westerners is being modified in the minds and hearts and actions of a growing number of people all over the world. Slowly, and at the same time the true believers were in charge and trying to kill everyone else, over the course of most of the Twentieth Century, the number of heretics has grown. Now even the believers are being influenced. Former jocks and nerds and nazis and managers and bosses and bureaucrats now practice meditation, exercise, contemplation of and with the senses, and contact, communication and openness to people with different beliefs. Slowly the wisdom of the heretics is integrated into the culture, but then becomes a set of beliefs and is defeated again. The mind converts experience to beliefs about experience. Constant practice of techniques for noticing allows for the continual rediscovery of experience, which is usually buried under a belief about the experience.

It appears that the maximally beneficial use of the human machine requires a constant reintegration of noticing and thinking. Thinking involves applying categories developed from previous noticing, and their constant upgrade only occurs when the continuous recurrence of noticing is possible, not limited by the previous set of beliefs.

For this reason, lucky for us, every belief system which cannot rapidly modify itself is falling apart. For this reason communism is falling apart. So is Catholicism. So is fundamentalism of all kinds. So is capitalism. Even experts are beginning to see that now. In our lifetimes most of us will witness many downfalls as a result of the coming to an end of the long-honored human habit of deification and blasphemous worship of organized belief systems. We have used them so well and so murderously throughout our history it's almost a pity to see them go. We have worshipped belief for untold millennia, since our genetic pathway diverged slightly from our brother chimpanzees. We are going to miss holy deification of belief terribly, but it is time we grew beyond that.

The only way to prepare your child for the future is to prepare her for that kind of future—one where there is nothing to truly believe in. It may not be as bad as we imagine. A new stage in evolution is occurring now. The genes have developed, at last, the capacity to modify themselves—it's called a brain/mind that doesn't believe itself to be sacred or absolute. It's a builder of models, a creator. Man the creator. This is the idea whose time has come. Hold on to your hat. There is no "up" to growing. The information age has arrived. In an information age you simply cannot prepare your children for the social and economic world they will live in by teaching them what to believe because it is impossible for you to know what that world will be like by the time they are twelve years old, much less when they are grown.

10 ❧ MORALISM

AS CHILDREN GROW UP THEY learn to abstract, generalize, and evaluate. They become emotionally attached to the summations and assessments they make in the course of learning how to make them. They learn to predict and control future events by remembering episodes that were painful and avoiding such episodes in the future. They remember episodes that were pleasant and try to recreate them. Life becomes a story, and the job is to remember the episodes, figure out the moral to the story, and use the instruction to live wisely and not get hurt or look like a fool. Growing up, children eventually get to the point where they can't stop living in their stories, and they continue, like compulsive gamblers, until they are finally exhausted or out of resources. This is moralism, a disease from which we all suffer. It is incurable. It can only be managed and lived with like herpes or diabetes.

Moralism, the disease, is not the same as simple morality. Moral values as guidelines for how to live are a necessity and a blessing. Rules of thumb, estimates of how best to proceed, and good guesses about directions to take based on past experiences of other people, are useful compasses to apply on our trip through life. Morality becomes moralism when the attachment to maintaining the story about how things should be blinds us to the extent that we can no longer see the way things are.

Most people believe that morals are good and children should be given moral instruction. Most people end up raising their children to live in the jail of moralism in which they themselves live. Most teachers consider their main function to be teaching children to behave and do right and be conscientious. Every adult has a whole raft of values they think should be taught to children. Few of these people are conscious of the way in which children are taught to value the values. Schools are central agents for transmission of the disease of moralism. The disease of moralism in adults is characterized by hysterical faith in the mind. We are all sick to death from moralism. The world of human beings may die from it.

The passing on of learning from one generation to the next is not a bad design, and as an evolutionary development, it seems to have triumphed. The idea-generating, self-perpetuating machine that has evolved seems to have worked. Human beings have taken over the world. The ability to act based on accumulated information, and to pass on great quantities of new information, is the primary survival characteristic of the most successful animal on earth. But, paradoxically, our survival mechanism may ultimately prove to be suicidal. It has allowed us to mass-produce the consumables that provide us with the comfortable lifestyles that eventually kill us, to develop a technology for mass destruction of the human and natural environment, and to rationalize the inexorable destruction of millions of lives relegated to the fate of poverty, disease, and violence. Now we have to fix a few of our own glitches, perhaps in just a decade or two, or risk dying of our own evolution. Otherwise, human history may become just a little blip in time at the end of which technical design ability surpassed psycho-emotional evolution, eventually extinguishing the species.

As Gregory Bateson said, in his calm, detached way, "Any species can get into an evolutionary cul-de-sac, and I suppose it is a mistake of sorts for that species to be a party to its own extinction. The human species, as we all know, may extinguish itself any day now."

We have arrived at the evolutionary crisis of moralism. Our chances of living beyond this crisis of consciousness are, of course, unknown. Probably the odds are in favor of extermination of either the species, or the world that provides the context in which it lives, or both.

MANAGING THE DISEASE OF MORALISM

Adult moralists are always angry people. The more the moralist is confronted with sloppy old experience, the more hysterical he or she becomes. We all get hysterical, but some of us lighten up and come to our senses more often than others. Some of us operate from hysterical moralism most of the time. Famous political moralists like Joseph McCarthy, Spiro Agnew, J. Edgar Hoover, and Hitler are great prototypes of the disease in our culture.

More lawyers have come to me for therapy than have members of any other profession, and it's not coincidence, since so much of their training is in learning to live by rules. One important rule they try to live by is that the proper way to be angry is to have a fight using the rules. They often try to do this in their private lives, with complete lack of success. Perpetual arguing to convince others of the rightness of your case doesn't work worth a damn in personal relationships, and we all know it but can't seem to stop. Thus, lawyers, what they learn, and how they end up, are an example of the disease of moralism worth pursuing. Let's take a look at what happens to these poor folks.

A law school education emphasizes the idiocy already built in by the culture, and makes for a good example of how not to do things. Law school education begins with memorizing torts—formally learning the cases from the past and the principles they represent—and it gets worse as it goes on. After three years of law school a graduate usually takes the next step toward a law career: the bar exam. For this he has to take a cram course to memorize cases, principles, generalizations, and values. When the exam is administered, the potential member of the bar knows in advance that he must score in the upper fifty percent of those taking the exam or fail. The standard requirement is that half must fail. In the District of Columbia, if you are in the lower half of the group, but close to the cut-off, you may appeal your grade and request that your paper be regraded. However, they will not tell you the new grade until after the next bar exam has been administered. If you want to be sure you can go to work as a lawyer, you had better take the exam again even though you may have passed already, once the regrade is completed. This is to teach you a lesson: do what you're told, no matter how ridiculous or unfair, if you want to be a lawyer. This continues, year after year, with the only apparent purpose being to make sure you have really learned to kiss ass in the culturally approved way.

Having passed the bar, if you are a high achiever, you then typically do a three- to seven-year stint of working seventy to eighty hours a week for a law firm trying to "make partner." After you have proven, through many additional trials, that you have learned to kiss ass in all circumstances, you may make partner. By the time you make partner you are a workaholic, so you keep up the pace out of habit, but also because you don't know what in the hell else to do in life but work and count principles. This is the group from which we choose our political representatives. This is where judges come from. Though the learned disease of moralism is rampant in all professions, the middle-aged lawyer is the quintessential prototype for this disease. Lawyers are the best representatives of the way people are today. They are the mind of our culture.

One of the things that helps this disease of moral hysteria to progress is our detachment from identification of ourselves as our experience. Hard physical work for the sake of survival used to keep more people in touch with the world of being. As life becomes less toil and more thinking and problem solving, there is less opportunity to have one's attention called forth from the mind by more immediate demands of survival on a day-to-day basis. The gap created by lack of grounding in our experience leaves us dependent on ideas, principles, rules, values, and imagination as our primary modes of orientation. These ideas and values are tightly held in the same way an adolescent grasps onto roles when he joins a gang or becomes a Christian or a Hare Krishna or falls in love and gets married in high school. Without roles and rules we fear we will lose control of ourselves. We will go crazy. We will lose our minds. The more intensely these rules and roles are defended, the further removed from grounding in experience the individual becomes.

After enough practice at role-playing and idealism, our whole way of orienting ourselves in the world depends on principles of orientation rather than on the ability to respond as needed based on what we perceive. This moralism, this web of entrapment of human aliveness, is a crippling disease. We all have it. It is terminal. It cannot be cured. It's a hell of a lot worse than herpes. It is as deadly as AIDS. It is in our schools. It is in our minds. It is in the bloodstream of our culture. It is in this book.

Sometimes I receive letters from people who have heard that I am an expert in stress management. They ask me to suggest what they can do about stress and various psychosomatic disorders. They want recommendations about how to behave and what to do. I know when I write back that whatever I tell them probably won't work. Whatever advice I give them will be used as another principle to beat themselves over the head with, which is what caused the problem in the first place. Moralists who read about ways to beat stress only make those ways into new rules with which to oppress themselves. People who try to make themselves have a bowel movement at 7:00 a.m. precisely, every day, whether they need to or not, are different from people who take a crap when they feel like they need to. J. Edgar Hoover died of apoplexy. Maybe he popped a blood vessel in righteous indignation. I like to imagine he was reading a book on stress management at the time.

FIELD INDEPENDENCE VERSUS FIELD DEPENDENCE

A number of experiments in the past thirty years have been designed to study what psychologists call "Field Dependence" and "Field Independence."

Imagine this scene: A person is seated in a darkened room. Ten feet in front of this person (the subject) stands another person holding a luminescent square frame surrounding a luminescent straight rod: The room is darkened; all the subject can see is the frame and the rod. Both the frame and the rod are mounted on an axle, so they may each be rotated in both directions. The person holding the frame and rod rotates both at random for a while. The frame is stopped and the rod continues moving for a while. The person holding the rod and frame then says to the subject, "Tell me when the rod is straight up and down, the same as the walls outside." Some people will make the rod straight up and down by using the square as a frame of reference. These people are called "field dependent" because they depend on the "context" or "field" provided by the frame, to judge when the rod is perpendicular. Other people line the rod straight up and down with regard to their own bodies, regardless of how the square is tilted. These people are called "field independent" because they operate independent of the square as a frame of reference.

Another variation of this experiment has the subject strapped into a tilting chair inside a room that tilts. Motors tilt both the room and chair and stop at some point at random. The subject strapped in the chair is instructed to give verbal instructions to the operator of the motor that moves the chair to make himself line up straight. Field dependent subjects will tolerate up to a 33-degree angle of tilt and will say, when questioned, that they are aligned with the walls outside as long as they are tilted in the same direction as the room. Like those who depend on the frame to judge the angle of the rod, these field-dependent people depend on the tilt of the room to adjust the tilt of the chair in which they sit, even though their own bodies are telling them they are not sitting upright.

There is further research that demonstrates that field dependence is correlated with social dependence. Field dependent, socially de-pendent people take their cues from external frames of reference.

Field independence is correlated with social independence and with creativity. Artists tend to be field independent. Those who learn, like lawyers, to depend on rules rather than the seats of their pants tend to be field dependent. Catholic parochial school is an excellent method for the accomplishment of field dependence. Parochial school students, like law students, make better sheep than people. Catholic education and law schools have provided me with a lot of miserable people as psychotherapy clients. I should be grateful. These people are looking for rescue from their educations. The problem is they all want me to tell them what to do, speaking as an authority who knows what they should do, so they can try hard to do it, be better than anyone else at it, and get good grades so God will love them.

Depending on an external frame of reference for social orienta-tion leads you to try to manipulate other people to get what you want rather than getting it on your own. What the well-trained field de-pendent client usually does is try to con the therapist into telling him to do what he already wants to do, but is afraid of failing at and get-ting blamed for the failure. That way, if he fails, he can blame the authority who told him to do it.

Fritz Perls said in 1946, "Principles are substitutes for an independent outlook. The owner would be lost in the ocean of events if he were not able to orient himself by these fixed bearings. Usually he is even proud of them and does not regard them as weaknesses, but as a source of strength. He hangs on to them because of the insufficiency of his own independent judgment." (*Ego, Hunger and Agression,* Gestalt Journal 1992.)

We are all afraid to give up our moralism. We are afraid that if we do we will go out of control. We might do something bad, or bizarre, or crazy. We might go out of our minds.

Erik Erikson, in the biography, *Young Man Luther* (Norton, 1993), speculates that: "Some day, maybe, there will exist a well-informed, well considered, and yet fervent public conviction that the most deadly of all possible sins is the mutilation of a child's spirit; for such mutilation undercuts the life principle of trust, without which every human act, may it feel ever so good and seem ever so right, is prone to perversion by destructive forms of conscientiousness."

When we take innocent and open children and train them to be moralists, we train them at one and the same time to be liars. Moralism and lying go hand in hand. "Being good" and "looking good," conscientiously valued, lead directly to lying. If you can fool the nuns into believing you are good like they want you to be, you can secretly do what you want. Moral instruction, stringently imposed, tears children loose from their grounding in experience, from their trust of the world based on just being here, and makes them into conscientious, suffering torturers of the next generation. In Erikson's words, "The child, forced out of fear to pretend that he is better when seen than when unseen, is left to anticipate the day when he will have the brute power to make others more moral than he ever intends to be himself."

The death-grip with which one holds on to principles is a source of unhappiness and anger. We can make a moral resolve that people should let up on themselves and other people, but that is just more

102

impotent moralism. If moralism is as common and influential in our society as I have described, how might one use the disease? That is, instead of attempting to cure it, how could we manage it and deal creatively with its power? Managing the disease of moralism is done by telling the truth like children do before they lose their innocence.

I have this disease. I want to use it rather than be used by it. How can I not just manage my critical, self-judgmental, mean-to-those-closest-to-me self, but use it to be happy, productive, and alive? My clients and friends and I have been having success in managing moralism by telling the truth. Children do this naturally. They play and pretend as well as describe, but they don't pretend that they are not pretending when they are. That is the difference between playing and lying. They know the difference until about adolescence and then lying becomes a part of the game.

The scary thing is that no one else can predict what will happen to you if you attempt to let up on your moralism. Only you can discover that, by abandoning the protection of your moralism in some way. Taking that risk is moving toward independence.

Self-reliance is field independence. Moral hysteria is field dependence. In the work I do, the most interesting questions are: Can someone who has learned to be field dependent and socially dependent learn independence? Can moralism be transformed from a life-threatening disease to a managed one? The answer to both questions is "Yes"—if the person is willing to tell the truth in a community of people who help each other stay sane—and "Yes"—if the person is raised by parents who tell the truth.

The reason I go into all of this to such an extent is that I think it is critical to your ability to parent that you disabuse yourself of any thought of teaching moral virtue to children, and allow them to grow up to at least ten or eleven years of age before you try to explain a lot of reasons for why they should behave in certain ways. You will only teach them moral hysteria and fear and how to fake understanding. You can stop them from doing things that might hurt them by just saying "No, you can't do that," but don't waste your breath explaining why if it takes more than one more sentence.

What children grow best on is love and attention and permission to experiment and learn from their experience. The upcoming section, which describes the next step, "Coming to an understanding of how the brain and mind work," is the evidence that supports that assertion.

Before we get to that, we need to clear ourselves by forgiving our heritage for the damage it has done to us, get over it, and go on.

11 ~ IN PRAISE OF THE OLD PARADIGM

THE TIME HAS COME TO say good-bye to the old paradigm of top-down management, the feudal system of top-down teaching, the autocracy of top-down parenting. It is time to have a funeral and to give our blessings and thanks to that human inventiveness into which we were born and which sustained us until it didn't anymore.

If we are to bury the old paradigm we must forgive all the bearers of the old ways. We must acknowledge our appreciation to all the workers, teachers, parents, politicians, and technicians for the wonderful heritage into which we were born. We must affirm all the fantastic technological gifts and benefits that have come from the intellectual pioneers who preceded us. We can, for good reason, be grateful for their creations and their sufferings and for all the modifications of the ideas and ideals they inherited that were changed through their experimentation with life, just as we are experimenting and creating in our own lives with what they gave us.

To all those people we must say our appreciations as well as our resentments and let bygones be bygones. We need to feel gratitude as a bodily experience, just as we need to feel resentment as a bodily experience, until we have experienced the experience and it has become, through our willingness and attention, a feeling of openness and presence to possibility again. So read and think and feel through this with me, and let's let go of our grudges and romantic soap-opera sentimentalizations about our heritage, so we can make a new beginning.

DEAR FOUR BEARS

Dear Forbears,

We appreciate you for all those solutions that worked in your lifetime. Even though they will not work for us anymore, and we have new insight about their pitfalls and side effects, we still thank you for building that last rung on the ladder we climbed up on.

Thanks to you for the Industrial Revolution, from which we now have the Information Age. Thank you for all the miserable wasted lives under top-down management that led to our current prosperity and comfort. Thanks to all the wage slaves and scrooges and people in between who lived their lives within the context of that perspective. Thanks to all the union organizers and good and bad cops and corrupt and decent politicians. Thanks to all the religious people and the warriors who defended beliefs to the death. Thanks to all the misguided educators and parents who brought this new chance into being. Thanks to all the alcoholics and factory workers and military personnel. We appreciate all of you for sacrificing your lives for us.

Thank you for all those nights of walking and rocking, when we were little, and all the hours you worked and all the care you showed, along with the abuse you propagated. Thanks for the abuse. Thanks for those hundreds of years of experimentation with altered states of consciousness when you had only alcohol to work with. Thanks for all those attempted celebrations of life, both those that worked out and those that didn't. Thanks for all the material goods and better food and better shelter and better toys. Thank you for all the shows on television, the good, the bad and the ugly. Thank you for all the moralism and the shoulds and the systems of self-torture you taught us. Thanks for that most-destructive-of-all Twentieth Century and all the bloodbaths from which we learned so much about malice afore-thought and malice after-thought and malice via thought.

Thanks for movies and television and technology. Thanks for all the images of romantic idealism and its corollary suffering. Thanks for the computer. Thanks for the cars and highways and buildings and cities and access to the countryside. Thanks for aviation and all its advances. Thanks for the exploration of outer space and the per-spective and technology it brought us. Thanks for video games and movie videos. Thanks for all the great radio shows and all the talk shows. Thanks for recorded music and CDs and for giving us access to the greatest moments of all the artists and performers of the world. Thanks for the Internet. Thanks to the framers of the Constitution of the United States and everyone who has helped put it into play and kept it alive.

Thanks for listening to the Native Americans who taught us so much that eventually became a part of our Constitution. Thanks for the "Great Books of the Western World" and for passing on to us the Great Conversation. Thank you for translating and teaching all the wisdom traditions of the East and of the Middle East in the second half of the Twentieth Century and all the practices that came from them. Thanks for all the mythologies of the world and for the evolu-tion of modern psychology. Thanks for all the poetry. Thanks for all the fiction. Thanks for all the drama. Thanks again for all the music. Thank you and goodbye.

12 ❧ THE MORAL ALTERNATIVE TO MORALISM

"Every child is an artist. The problem is how to remain an artist after he grows up."

—PABLO PICASSO

MORALISM IS A DISEASE OF attachment to principles out of fear of loss of control. It is an illness often treated by those of us who work in the helping professions and particularly by Radical Honesty trainers and therapists. We are not opposed to moral values or morality. We even have a few moral principles ourselves. It's the intensity of attachment to moral righteousness that is the sickness, not the valuing of some ideas and behaviors over others. In fact, we hold, as a moral value, the unlearning of excessive attachment to principles that in so many instances has become self-crippling.

The age-old argument between advocates of moral correctness and punishment and the advocates of love and forgiveness is carried on in daily life. This argument is illustrated in the story in the Bible in which one of Jesus's disciples picked grain on the Sabbath and was criticized by the Pharisees because it was "work" and it was against the rules of God to work on the Sabbath. Jesus said something like "the law was made for man, man was not made for the law." In other words, the law was created to serve man. Man was not created in order to serve the law. The primacy of love as an organizing principle, over principle as an organizing principle, has been addressed by some recent scientific research. This research changes the argument by putting the learning of love and the learning of the mind in a sequence in time, developmentally, rather than in opposition to each other. The saying everyone learns from evolutionary biology, that "ontogeny recapitulates phylogeny" has always seemed intuitively true. That our evolutionary development as a species is duplicated in the first months in the womb has been confirmed with many examples and detailed photography of fetuses at various stages of development. Now it appears that developing new capacities continues with brain development beyond the womb and into the first several years of life. Neural pathways continue to be formed and the brain continues to grow and its capacities to expand for many years. This process can be helped or hurt by the way the child is treated.

A GENERAL THEORY OF LOVE

I want to review in more detail the wonderful little book I referred to earlier, *A General Theory of Love.* The authors, Thomas Lewis, Fari Amini and Richard Lannon, three psychiatrists—at least one of whom is a damned good writer—summarize and eloquently contribute to the advancement of our wisdom about love: where it comes from, how it evolved, what it has to do with the structure and operation of the brain itself, and particularly how the programming and growth of neural pathways during childhood are critical to the ultimate capacity for successful human life individually and in groups. Here is a selected list of excerpts from several chapters from that book, along with a few comments of my own. I do this in order to hit the high points of this marvelous book, but don't let this keep you from reading the whole thing. The implications of this book for parenting are immense and I will, of necessity, miss some of them in this review.

To start with, the authors take on the task of looking for love in the brain, literally. They talk of modern neurophysiology and the evolution of the brain in mammals and the brain's primary function of contributing to survival. Then they look for the seat of love in that "symphony of signaling neurons" called the brain. They point out that we human beings have three brains in one, and that we can look at the addition of one brain on top of the other as a way to trace stages of development in our evolutionary history. The reptilian brain, "a bulbous elaboration of the spinal cord," handles the baseline functions of vital control: "breathing, swallowing, . . . heartbeat . . . visual tracking system . . . startle center." Next comes, "Humanity's second or limbic brain [which] drapes itself around the first with languid ease." The limbic brain came into being when "early mammals evolved from small, lizardish reptiles . . . [and developed] the peculiar mammalian innovation—carrying developing young within a warm-blooded body rather than leaving them outside in eggs." The third brain, the neocortex, is made up of "two symmetrical sheets, each the size of a large, thick linen napkin, and each crumpled for better cramming into the small oblate shell of the skull." Of this brain they say, " . . . science has made some progress at mapping the functions and capacities of this massed neuronal army. Speaking, writing, planning and reasoning all originate in the neocortex. So do the experience of our senses, what we know as awareness, and our conscious motor control, what we know as will."

The brain in the middle of things, so to speak, the limbic brain, warrants a closer look for its ramifications for child rearing. It appears that, in fact, limbic learning is probably at least of equal importance to intellectual learning, particularly in the early months of life, and perhaps throughout childhood. We might even go so far as to say that without a clear intention to value limbic learning in the early years of life, the central core of organization for later use of the neocortex as well as the limbic brain could be impaired.

The evolutionary perspective gives us an immediate intuitive understanding of where the beginning of learning about love comes from: "As mammals split off from the reptilian line, a fresh neural structure blossomed within their skulls. The brand-new brain transformed not only the mechanics of reproduction (giving birth to babies, not eggs) but also the organismic orientation toward offspring. Detachment and disinterest mark the parental attitude of the typical reptile, while mammals…bear their young live; they nurse, defend, and rear them while they are immature. Mammals, in other words, take care of their own. Rearing and care taking are so familiar to humans that we are apt to take them for granted, but these capacities were once novel—a revolution in social evolution. The most common reaction a reptile has to its young is indifference; it lays its eggs and walks (or slithers) away. Mammals form close-knit mutually nurturant social groups—families—in which members spend time touching and caring for each other." The limbic brain also characteristically has a couple of more functions. It "permits mammals to sing to their children…and mammals can play with one another." The limbic brain appears to be where love first evolved and the seat of where love now occurs. Even more important is the apparent fact that the new limbic brain is where love is learned—and it may be that for the neural connections even to develop so that a person has the capacity to love, the limbic brain must be nurtured by another limbic-brained being or beings (including pets). It may be that if we skip over the importance of this in our educational and parenting values, we do so at our own and our children's peril. *We have, as our cultural history evolved, come to over-value intellectual learning, and while attending to that, particularly with young children, we may have been missing the boat on an even more critical capacity.*

A COMMON MISTAKE OF THE RATIONAL MIND—
THINKING TOO HIGHLY OF ITSELF

In the attempt to integrate and coordinate the functions of all three brains, each human being and each social group of human beings has a few possible pitfalls to face, not the least of which is the one just mentioned of overvaluing our neocortical functions—our capacity for thought—and slighting the abilities and functions and development of the other brains.

The following excerpt from the same authors is, I think, critical to understanding the necessity of interrupting a western cultural aberration we are all living in, for the sake of our own children. "In humans, the neocortical capacity for thought can easily obscure other, more occult, mental activities. Indeed, the blazing obviousness of cognition opens the way to a pancognitive fallacy: I think, therefore everything I am is thinking. But in the words of a neocortical brain as mighty as Einstein's: 'We should take care not to make the intellect our God; it has, of course, powerful muscles, but no personality. It cannot lead. It can only serve.'" Summarizing this point, the authors go on to say, "Words, good ideas, and logic mean nothing to at least two brains out of three. Much of one's mind does not take orders. . . . Emotional life can be influenced but it cannot be commanded." The authors of *A General Theory of Love* tell us that the limbic brain is an independent source of information the neocortical mind has trouble figuring out. "Like the art it is responsible for inspiring, the limbic brain can move us in ways beyond logic that have only the most inexact translations in a language the neocortex can comprehend . . . Frost wrote that a poem 'begins as a lump in the throat, as sense of wrong, a homesickness, a love sickness. It is never a thought to begin with.' . . . Neither does love begin with a thought."

So let's assume, for the sake of argument, that when being loved informs a young mind about what to do with itself, that works better than a mind informing love about what to do with itself. In the words of Jacob Needleman "We think we can play with love, but we are mistaken. Love plays with us." (*A Little Book on Love,* Doubleday, 1996)

WHAT DOES THIS HAVE TO DO WITH CHILD-REARING?

I said before that if we look at what is universal about humans we have a chance of transcending limiting cultural values. Facial expressions, for example, appear to be universal. Again, I quote from *A General Theory of Love:* "Facial expressions are identical—all over the globe, in every culture and every human being ever studied. No society exists wherein people express anger with the corners of the mouth going up, and no person has ever lived who slits his eyes when surprised. An angry person appears angry to everyone worldwide and likewise a happy person, and a disgusted person."

The beginning of learning this universal skill is right after childbirth, and it is related to a learning that preceded it in the womb: "...babies remember their mother's voice and face within thirty-six hours of birth. Within days an infant recognizes and prefers not only his mother's voice but also her native language, even when spoken by a stranger. You might think this knowledge comes from postpartum interactions—quick learning indeed. But a newborn doesn't recognize his father's voice, indicating that neonatal preferences reflect learning before birth. The auditory system's rapid development *in utero* and the watery womb's excellent sound system surround the fetus in a symphony. . . . Facial expressions, tone of voice, and touch carry a mammal's emotional messages; ...a baby is born fluent in that signaling system." For this reason, lots of parents have the dad talking to the baby with his head on Mama's tummy, during the last few months of pregnancy. Mom may also talk and sing to the baby. I don't know if it helps the baby or not, but it helps the parents and I don't think it can hurt. It could put a few new bells and whistles on the welcome wagon to life. "Just as grammatical English emerges from our lips automatically, a structured pattern of emotional relatedness emanates from each of us. We play out our unconscious knowledge in every unthinking gesture we make in the dance of loving. If a child has the right parents, he learns the right principles—that love means protection, care taking, loyalty, sacrifice. He comes to know it not because he is told, but because his brain automatically narrows crowded confusion into a few regular prototypes."

One terrible mistake that moralistic rule-givers and punishers and trainers of children make, is to try to tell children what is right, or scare them into doing it rather than simply showing them by example. Teachers and parents teach the most critical skill a human being can have by how loving they are with kids—by how they *be* with the child. The way children are cared for is critical to early brain development as well as future capacity—both social and intellectual. According to these modern neuroscientists, " . . . love alters the structures of our brains." Then once the structures are in place, repeated emotional experiences form a kind of thematic programming system that makes us available or unavailable for future emotional possibilities. (See *Practicing Radical Honesty,* Blanton, Sparrowhawk Press, 2000)

EARLY ESTABLISHMENT OF PATTERNS FOR EMOTIONAL PROPENSITIES

The authors continue, " . . . the evanescence of emotions, their pulse-and-fade propensity, is nearly musical. Now the metaphor draws closer. A musical tone makes physical objects vibrate at its frequency, the phenomenon of sympathetic reverberation. A soprano breaks a wineglass with the right note as she makes unbending glass quiver along with her voice. Emotional tones in the brain establish a living harmony with the past in a similar way. . . . When an emotional chord is struck, it stirs to life past memories of the same feeling . . . A childhood replete with suffering lingers in the mind as bitter, encoded traces of pain. Even a tangential reminder of that suffering can spur the outbreak of unpleasant thoughts, feelings, and anticipations. As if he had bumped a sleeping guard dog, the adult who was an abused child may feel the fearsome jaws of memory close after he glimpses a mere intimation of his former circumstance. In a sad empirical confirmation, maltreated children flipping through pictures of faces exhibit a hugely amplified brain wave when they encounter an angry expression."

As replicated memories of emotion deepen patterns of experienced and anticipated feelings, they generate an ever-present tendency to notice new things, not neutrally, but in a kind of expectant search for new information that fits the previously existing model. Teams of prototypes, developed from repeated emotional experience, become a network—what the authors call an Attractor. "A network then registers novel sensory information as if it conformed to past experience. In much the same way, our sun's blinding glare washes countless dimmer stars from the midday sky."

Remember, these are neural patterns, and the older we get the more of them we have. The implications of this are staggering. All of us, every day, are feeling things triggered by, but not necessarily pertinent to, the present circumstances, except for a kind of "clang" association with some past emotional pattern of experiences. This results in our not only feeling things that are not pertinent, but also missing things that are going on while our attention is absorbed in the associated memory. We spend time actually feeling, seeing, and hearing things that are not there anymore. These things that are not there fill in the blanks of what we miss in real life while we are daydreaming about the past.

It is hard to overestimate the importance of this assertion. Many times every day we hear things that are not there. While doing that, we miss hearing the things that actually occur while we are re-experiencing the past. We see things that do not happen. We miss seeing things that do happen. Then we fill in the blanks in the information resulting from our inattention with the illusionary pre-figured sounds and sights and feelings from the past. *Essentially, we are constantly modifying our ongoing experience of life and fitting it in with what we have learned to expect and guard against.*

116

All of us who have been in big arguments with others about something that happened and what it meant (namely everyone who has ever been in a relationship with another human being) know that other people's minds simply can't be trusted. Sometimes we even suspect the same about our own. What we don't do is build couples, families and communities to keep ourselves straight based on admitting that our own information is as suspect as everyone else's. This is why I say: A mind is a terrible thing! Waste it!

If we actually get, in our bones, that we ourselves are not as reliable as we think we are—we don't remember everything perfectly, we don't always know what's going on, we're not always in control—it is not necessarily a bad thing. It can lead to a strong relationship based on mutual vulnerability in a couple, and loving parents who can forgive their children, and good families and strong communities of mutual support. We are all imperfect here together.

Most of us like to think we are maintaining control at all times by knowing what's going on. While we maintain that illusion, the influence of Attractors that draw us to some people and make us want to avoid others, is strong. Because you love your child, for example, you have warm predispostion for anything they do. Your children, especially when they are really young, most of the time, can do no wrong. You build records of loving them, and have a predisposition to notice behavor that justifies wonderful assessments of them and to ignore behavior others might not find laudable. Because of your Attractors, when you are loving them, based on past behavior and loving experiences with them, everything they do is just wonderful. Then when they get to be teenagers and break through your model of who they are based on the past, you are mad at them a lot more, and sometimes the reverse becomes true. It seems terribly unfair that that wonderful child, who used to love you has become such a selfish, inconsiderate brat, who wishes you weren't around to bother her. She reminds you of the teenagers who snubbed you when you were a teen. Old

Attractors are triggered and you are off to the races in your mind again.

The reason I recommend Radical Honesty throughout the whole life of parenting is that you have to be "out loud" about what you feel and what meaning you are making at the time to have even a slim chance of communicating, at both limbic and cognitive levels, as both parent and child continue to grow. You have to share with each other, and the family, and the extended family, and the community of friends, for the sake of ongoing corrections. When we can all acknowledge that we don't know what we are doing, but might discover how to "parent" together, and "child" together, and "family" together as we go along, we have a slim chance of being less dysfunctional than the families we grew up in.

Things can get even more confusing in blended families. Think of the problems of co-parenting and step parenting and being children in composite families when clashing memories are triggered. Reactions based on past experiences with other sets of parents and siblings emerge. Everyone enters into relationships by placing new sets of people into old roles. There are both positive and negative Attractors in all relationships. That means that in reaction to neural patterns formed in earlier relationships with people, say, of the same sex as the one you are currently in relationship with, you have things that draw you to this person and things that repel you at the same time. How confusing! It's the same for the kids in relation to the new step-parent and siblings, and usually to two sets of parents or step-parents!

One thing we can depend on is that we are all in the same boat. It might seem humiliating at first, but we must admit this to each other. We can't see our own blind spots. They can't see their own blind spots. We can feel a relatedness limbically with a mate, and our kids can simply not get it, or feel quite the opposite. Because of the fundamental unreliability of minds, only when parenting involves permission for people to feel whatever they feel, think whatever they think, be however they be, and do it all out loud, can the mutually impaired but deluded group of human beings, known for the time being as a family, work things out! What you have to give up, in order to be a halfway decent parent is the idea that you are right all the time, just because you're the parent! (Can you remember how many times you wanted to say this to your own parents?) This is hard to do for most of us. Practice in getting over our own righteousness with our own parents, and in other relationships, is what helps the most.

These authors say, "Because human beings remember with neurons, we are disposed to see more of what we have already seen, hear anew what we have heard most often, think just what we have always thought . . . No individual can think his way around his own Attractors, since they are embedded in the structure of thought."

Isn't that just awful?

Wait. It gets worse:

"And in human beings an Attractor's influence is not confined to its mind of origin. The limbic brain sends an Attractor's sphere of influence exploding outward with the exuberance of a nova's gassy shell. Because limbic resonance and regulation join human minds together in a continuous exchange of influential signals, every brain is part of a local network that shares information—including Attractors . . . All of us, when we engage in relatedness, fall under the gravitational influence of another's emotional world, at the same time we are bending his emotional mind with ours."

Damn!

Wait. It gets worse yet:

"The reach of limbic Attractors stretches beyond the moment. The *sine qua non* of a neural network is its penchant for strengthening neuronal patterns in direct proportion to their use. The more often you do or think or imagine a thing, the more probable it is that your mind will revisit its prior stopping point . . . Ongoing exposure to one person's Attractors does not merely activate neural patterns in another—it also strengthens them. Long-standing togetherness writes permanent changes into a brain's open book.

"In a relationship, one mind revises another; one heart changes its partner. This astounding legacy of our combined status as mammals and neural beings is limbic revision: the power to remodel the emotional parts of the people we love, as our Attractors activate certain limbic pathways, and the brain's inexorable memory mechanism reinforces them."

Well (thank Limbic!), this is not such bad news. It means that psychotherapy can work. It means that a therapeutic community in which people tell the truth and work things out can be curative to someone suffering from a limiting set of emotional patterns. People can actually form new patterns, as well as make new sense out of the past confusion. It means families can heal. It means people can change.

"Who we are and who we become depends, in part, on whom we love." And vice versa! Herein lies the possibility of great communities and great movements. But here lies, equally, the possibility of mass insanity.

Human beings are indeed strange creatures. And their capacity for extreme aberration as well as extreme courage may come, literally, from the same location in the brain, where emotional patterns exist that we are barely aware of, and seldom honestly share. I think it is safe to say that whole cultures share limbic sets, and intellectual rationales to match them. Let's take a look at an historically significant negative case.

If we think of Hitler as a personality organized around a certain limited set of limbic patterns, who had a particular resonance with the people of his day and time, we can see that whatever intellectual rationalization was used for an apparent organizing principle didn't matter much. It was the limbic resonance. That resonance may have been there because of previous cultural suffering all those people had in common (childhoods during and after WW1), or child-rearing patterns in that culture, or both, or those and a number of other factors.

THE WORK OF STANLEY MILGRAM

I first heard about a social psychologist named Stanley Milgram when he presented a review of his research, conducted at Yale University, to a meeting of the American Psychological Association in Chicago in 1965. Milgram was given an award by one branch of the Association, while being censured by another branch, on the same day, for the same research. Here is how he got praised and in trouble:

Milgram had, several years earlier, read a book by Hannah Arendt about the trial of Adolf Eichmann, Hitler's infamous director of operations, who had been responsible for overseeing the executions of most of the six million Jews and other people judged unacceptable by the Third Reich. Hannah Arendt, who had covered the war crimes trial for The New Yorker magazine and several American newspapers, reported that Eichmann's defense was that he should not be held personally responsible for a crime against mankind because he was doing his duty in the social system of which he was a part. His lawyers argued that a court might judge that the social system was criminal, but not the person doing his duty within that social system. This argument was rejected. Eichmann's adjudicators concluded that he was individually responsible for the crimes he committed, regardless of the social system of which he was a part, and he was executed.

Hannah Arendt then raised another question, which fascinated Stanley Milgram. Was Adolf Eichmann some unusual social deviant, some sadistic exception to common humanity, or was he just an ordinary bureaucrat? Arendt pointed out that only twice in his entire career had he actually witnessed an execution, which, he said, he found "repugnant." What he actually did was shuffle papers in an office and make phone calls and give orders. Outside of work, he seemed to have a normal life with family and friends and associates. Was he normal?

Milgram designed an experiment to see if he could somewhat simulate the conditions in which Eichmann operated. He drew a random stratified sample of males from the community around Yale. (In later versions of the original study he included females, and found no significant differences between males and females in the results of the experiment.) He paid each subject, in advance, seven dollars for participating in an experiment that he told them was "a study of the effects of negative reinforcement on learning."

When Milgram met his subjects, he used a room in a building on the campus of Yale University. He wore a white lab coat and introduced himself as Dr. Milgram. There were three people in the room: Milgram and two others, both of whom were apparently participants in the study. Only one of them, however, was a true subject—the second, unbeknownst to the first, was a stooge, a student actor from the drama department. Milgram said to them, "I am conducting a study of the effects of negative reinforcement on learning. In this study, one of you will be the teacher and one will be the learner. I will flip a coin to see which is which." The coin flip was rigged, so that the true subject from the sample was always the "teacher."

After the coin flip, Milgram led both subjects into a room containing a very large and impressive electric chair, and proceeded to strap the learner (the stooge) into the chair and apply electrodes to his wrists and head. In later versions of the experiment (the experiment was run several times with several groups of subjects before being written up in journals and reported to the American Psychological Association), Milgram mentioned in passing that he was using electrode paste "to keep the flesh from being burnt," and the learner/stooge mentioned in passing that he had a "slight heart condition."

Then the "teacher" (who was the true subject) was led to a room with a one-way mirror so that he could see the person in the electric chair but the person could not see him. He was seated in front of a panel of thirty switches, which were labeled clearly in 15-volt increments from 15 volts to 450 volts. Above the switches were verbal labels in gradations of degree: "shock," "dangerous shock," "severely dangerous shock;" and two steps before the last switch was an ambiguous but ominous "XXXX." Milgram said, "I am going to project a list of words on the wall in front of the person in the chair. He will be given several repetitions of the word list to learn it. When he sees a word appear on the wall, his task will be to name the next word from the list before it is projected, based on having memorized the list. If he makes a mistake, I want you to administer an electric shock, and I would like you to increase the voltage of this shock in fifteen-volt increments. Do you understand the instructions?" When the "teacher" fully understood the instructions, the experiment began.

The stooge in the chair was only receiving a cue every time a switch was thrown, but the "teacher" didn't know that. As the "learner" made mistakes and was "shocked," he reacted more and more dramatically. At first he just jumped a little. As the shocks progressed he began jumping and yelling out. Then he started screaming when he was shocked. Then he began screaming and saying he wanted to stop. Then he said, "Stop this! I want out! Whoever is doing this stop! I want to quit!" Then as the voltage got closer to the end, two steps before the end, the "learner" screamed, convulsed, and collapsed completely. When the next word appeared and there was no response, Milgram said, "We'll have to count that an error; shock him again." Then one more time, no response, "That's an error; shock him again." In order to get to the end of the row of switches the teacher had to shock the learner two more times while he was apparently completely unconscious.

Prior to actually conducting the study, Milgram had given a questionnaire to a similar random stratified sample of people from the community around Yale in which he asked if the respondents "would ever purposely inflict pain on a fellow human being, regardless of the social circumstances." Over ninety-two percent said that they would not. When he ran the actual experiment, however, sixty-eight percent of the people went all the way to the top. The "teachers" sweated excessively; some cried, some went into hysterical laughter. Many, even though debriefed and told that it was an act, reported, when interviewed two weeks later, that they had had nightmares about what they had done. The subjects obviously had a very hard time doing what they did, but nevertheless did it. They resisted, they felt bad about it, they felt guilty, but they did what they were told. Milgram had written down, in advance, four statements he could make in response to objections on the part of the "teacher"—the strongest one being: "The experiment must go on."

Later, Milgram pointed out that this experiment was not really fair to Adolf Eichmann because Eichmann had many colleagues who cooperated in his bureaucracy. So Milgram modified his experiment by adding one more stooge, a person in the room with the teacher who pulled a master switch to "turn on the electricity" each time an error was made. When the responsibility or blame could be shared with just one other person in this way, ninety-two percent of the subjects went all the way to the top.

Milgram's presentation was called "A Study in the Legitimation of Evil" and he concluded about the people in his sample, and by generalization the people in the culture from which his sample had come: "Individuals will generally go against their own moral inclinations in order to cooperate with authority."

No sub-group in the sample differed in a statistically significant way from the norm of the whole population. Women did not differ from men, and groupings by ethnic origin, religious orientation, age, and so on were not significantly different. One group approached statistical significance—Catholics—and that difference was in the direction of more cooperation with authority rather than less. Having seen lots of recovering Catholics from parochial schools in my private practice of psychotherapy, this does not surprise me.

One of the things I like about this study is that none of us knows how we would have fared. We would all like to think that we would have been in the eight percent who refused to go on. But obviously, not all of us could have been in the eight percent. There were some few subjects who not only quit but proceeded to speak to the provost at Yale and to Milgram himself, demanding that Milgram stop not only that particular experiment but stop experimenting period. We would all like to think we would have been one of them. Most of us would have cooperated and felt bad about it, but cooperated nevertheless. Most of us would simply have overruled our limbic brain with the neocortically learned "respect for authority."

I have been fascinated with this work for thirty-six years. I used to report on Milgram's work in speeches I made against the war in Vietnam. Much of my work as a group leader and psychotherapist has been an attempt to discover and reinforce the kind of independent individuality that might allow for those statistics to change.

I think, that in order to demonstrate their independence in the circumstance of that experiment, it was necessary for individuals to be able to act according to their compassion—their identification as one being to another with the person in the electric chair. Their compassion made them "feel bad" about what they did, but it was not enough to overrule their training in obedience to authority. Their compassion would have to have been stronger than their need to obey the professor from Yale in the white lab coat. Their sense of individual responsibility and the courage to act upon it would have to have been stronger than their years of training from school and church and family to acquiesce to authority. The integrity of their own feelings would have to have been more powerful in determining their actions than their moral obligation to not challenge the constituted authority or rock the boat of the existing power structure. To put this in the terminology we have adopted from *A General Theory of Love,* the feelings emanating from their limbic brain would have to have taken precedence over their authority-trained rational mind seated in the neocortex.

Eichmann was just an average guy. Average guys are just Eichmanns. So are average gals. As Milgram chillingly told "60 Minutes" in 1979,

"If a system of death camps were set up in the United States of the sort we had seen in Nazi Germany, one would be able to find sufficient personnel for those camps in any medium-sized American town." Most of us would obey Hitler like most did in Nazi Germany. Most of us still are obeying some questionably constituted authority, instead of acting on our own authority, most of the time. Most of us have lined up to go to recess and lined up to come back into the classroom and lined up to go to lunch and lined up to come back from lunch and sat in rows and not talked and waited in lines and behaved and waited for the bell to ring and are still doing that.

Most of us operate from models of what we should and should not do rather than our feelings, our preferences, and what we feel called forth to do based on our empathetic connections with other human beings. For the most part, we have organized our world to keep it that way. As the Sufis say, ninety-eight per cent of humanity spends ninety-eight per cent of their time at the level of consciousness which they call "the level of belief." We have been rewarded and punished and inspired and controlled and conditionally loved enough to form lots of Attractors that incline us towards obedience to authority regardless of how badly we feel about what we are doing to a fellow human being. The question I want to ask you is: Do you really want to raise your child to be this way?

HONORING BEING

Use your own imagination: What would a society organized around values that honor being, rather than obedience to authority, be like? What would a family organized around values that honor being, rather than obedience to authority, be like? What changes might occur in how we operate together if we had a world, or family or school, organized around honoring the being of others, rather than mere order? Can't we think of the limbic brain, in fact, as our equipment for appreciating being? What might be different if we paid attention to love as a social organizational principle? What if we valued child-rearing more than contracts, for example?

We might set a maximum wage of $5 an hour for lawyers because legal work is not all that important, and a minimum of $300 an hour for child care workers because encouraging children to remain in touch with being, by being loved and honored by another, bigger being, is so much more important than the work of lawyers. Childcare workers and parents and teachers, who are more in touch with children because of their love of the being of young beings, would be getting lawyers' fees, and lawyers would be getting the minimum wage. Perhaps our legal work could be done by illegal immigrants. The world would be quite a different place if we valued compassion more than obedience and order, and we put our money where our values were. If, in fact, we were to honor our limbic abilities more than authority, could not this big family we call humanity become less dysfunctional altogether?

DRIVING THE LIMBIC LIMO AND LEARNING THE LIMBIC LIMBO

I am a limbic detective. I have spent my life as a Sherlock Holmes of emotional life. I have been fascinated all my life with life stories. I like to look at people's pictures of themselves as children and have them tell me what it was like for them then, as well as they can remember. I am fascinated with the question: "How did that child become this person?" So I cannot help but love the topic the authors of *A General Theory of Love* devoted a chapter to: " . . . how aspects of parental love shape a young mind." How can we learn to love in a way that transcends the limitations of the cultural, emotional and intellectual programming we have been exposed to in our own years of growing up? One place to start on this, both to heal parents and to give a good start to children, is the family bed. This is considered innovative in terms of our modern world, but it is actually older than humanity. Take a breath now. We will pursue the implications of the family bed for our vision of a new kind of world in the next chapter.

Step IV

Come to an Understanding of How the Brain and the Mind Work

13 ⌒ THE FAMILY BED—
A LIMBIC SERVICE STATION

My WIFE, AMY, AND I raised our two children to sleep in a family bed for about the first six years of their lives. We all loved snuggling together in that big king-sized bed and our kids learned a lot about how to love by doing so. I think learning to love is critical to learning to think. Both of our children are geniuses. I think that is because of the beginning context of love, from which they had the opportunity to learn other important things.

There are many advocates of holding, touching, nursing, playing, sleeping and snuggling together, and some of their books are listed in the bibliography of this book. *The Family Bed* by Tine Thevenin (1975) and *The Continuum Concept,* (Jean Liedloff 1985) mentioned several other times in this book, have been particularly influential.

Our culture's objections to the family bed have to do with cultural paranoia about children becoming sexually aroused when in bed with parents, probably instigated by Sigmund Freud and his later American followers. Somehow we came up with a rule that damages all our children, and probably actually kills some of them. As Lewis, et. al. say, "The American habit of sleeping separately is a global and historical singularity. Almost all the world's parents sleep with their children, and until the last sliver of human history, separate sleep was surpassingly rare." The U.S. has "the highest incidence of sudden infant death syndrome (SIDS) in the world: two deaths for every thousand live births . . . human societies with the lowest incidence of SIDS are also the ones with widespread co-sleeping."

One objection to the family bed is the lost opportunity for sex. That can be taken care of several ways. First off, you can have sex in the bed without waking the baby during that first year. Put a pillow between you two and the baby and go to it. You may get interrupted, or wake the baby, or have the baby triggered to wake up by the smells and sounds. We don't actually know what effect the parents' making love nearby has on the baby's consciousness.

Apparently, in cultures where sex is less taboo, children who see, hear and smell their parents and others having sex grow up just fine. The solution I prefer, given that we have more taboos about sex than you can shake a stick at, so to speak, is for the parents to have another place in the house to go to in order to make love, after the children are asleep in the family bed. Do it on the altar of your meditation room. Do it in the room you have set up for the child to move into when he leaves the family bed. Make a special place where the two of you can retreat to make love or talk. This can be an opportunity for fun rather than a burden.

The culture you live in has established expectations about how young couples are supposed to have close contact with their kids at night. It goes against all of evolutionary history for mammals and for humans. Evolutionary sociobiologists and psychologists recommend that human parents sleep with their kids for at least the first year or so of their lives. I recommend that you do it until the kids want a room of their own, which is usually at about six or seven years of age. Whether you do it for that long or not, in infancy it seems to be really important.

Again, I quote from *A General Theory of Love:* "Sleep is an intricate brain rhythm, and the neurally immature infant must first borrow the patterns from parents ... The steady piston of an adult heart and the regular tidal waves coordinate the ebb and flow of young internal rhythms."

Now here is the most important quote from that book for all of us American and American-influenced westerners who are raising children. Not only is this beautifully spoken, it is confirmation of the core theme of Radical Parenting. It also clearly contradicts current folk wisdom that justifies a lot of child abuse "for their own good."

"The family bed debate dances around an American conundrum: we cherish individual freedom more than any society, but we do not respect the process whereby autonomy develops. Too often, Americans think that self-rule can be foisted on someone in the way a traveler thrusts a bag at a bellhop: compel children to do it alone, and they'll learn how; do it with them and spawn a tentacled monster that knows only how to cling. In truth, premature pressure stunts the genuine, organic capacity for self-directedness that children carry within them. Independence emerges naturally not from frustrating and discouraging dependence, but from satiating dependence. Children rely heavily on parents, to be sure. And when they are done depending, they move on—to their own beds, houses, and lives."

FAMILYING IS A VERB

I like that quote so much because in my experience as a psychotherapist, co-dependent people, who try constantly to force others to take care of them, are compensating for the way their parents failed to let them be dependent when they were young and it was appropriate to do so. In order to not make this mistake, a good rule of thumb about how to treat your kids is this question: How much fun is this for me and my mate and the kids? If it is fun and nobody gets hurt too bad, go for it. What seems to be most common to the memories folks who are needy all the time is that their parents were not fun. They were serious. They had standards. They had a lot of requirements for how you had to act. That's no fun. Not only is it not fun, but the kids will make damn sure they do the opposite of what you are enforcing in order to get back at you.

Famlying is an ongoing activity, done moment to moment, and there is a great possibility for joy at any moment. If the limbic patterns you established with your own parents were joyful and nurturing the job is easier. If they were not, you need to complete your unfinished emotional business with your parents and establish a new pattern with your partner or partners in familying. You can provide for yourself and your mate a kind of job corps retraining program in limbic development. This means getting over things you have emotionally avoided completing with your parents, and forgiving them for the mistakes they made when they didn't know what they were doing. It also means learning how to forgive your mate over and over again by acknowledging and telling the truth about your feelings, and listening when your mate does the same. Reading my other books, *Radical Honesty* and *Practicing Radical Honesty,* or attending any of the Radical Honesty Workshops, or being in a Radical Honesty Practice Group, can be a lot of help.

LET'S GET DUMBER TOGETHER

If we are to take what we are finding out about how human beings evolved and use it to learn how to live together and be happier and have a good time familying, we need to get dumber, in a way, rather than smarter. We need to be neocortically liberated and limbically alive.

If you aren't, you can heal much of the damage. That is what psychotherapy and good group work is for. That is what the therapeutic community of family and friends help with. If you have been walking with a slight limbic, you can fix it by paying careful attention to your experience of being with and sharing with other people. Go out on a limbic. Learn from the Buddha, a limbic lunatic. Take other limbicational opportunities. If you were raised by a mom with a schedule in one hand and a clock in another, you don't have to sing "the limbically impaired momma blues" all your life. Wax limbical. Let compassion go to your head.

Pair up with other couples with children and form the limbic liberation front. You can practice a kind of limbic yoga by sharing with them. This can make up for limbic deprivation during childhood, and keep you from passing on the limbically deprived heritage of the culture you were born into. The family bed kills two birds with one stone because it begins your rehabilitation, as well as providing a better beginning for your kids than you had.

14 ✍ WHAT IS A MIND AND HOW CAN YOU CLEAR IT?

I KNOW YOU COULD TELL your own parents what they could have, and should have, done differently. Particularly now, after we have given some pretty good scientific validation of how right you are about how wrong they were. If you can get them to read this book and have a conversation about child-rearing with them that goes beyond just making them wrong, you all might have the possibility of mutually loving each other and enjoying raising your own children in a whole new way. You might be able to have give your children an altogether different set of complaints about how they were raised! That's probably what progress looks like.

You and your mate and source family and friends have the possibility of transcending your collective past by asking each other a number of questions that allow you to see through your cultural and family blind spots: How do you get out of your own way in order to live a more powerfully loving and nurturing life with your child? How do you keep your mind's patterned reactions from your own childhood (which are triggered by the very existence of your child) from getting in your way?

The first step to discovery and invention of an answer to these questions is to acknowledge how you DO get in your own way. How do you block yourself or interfere with yourself? How do you shoot yourself in the foot before the race is over? How do you talk to yourself, coach yourself, warn yourself, worry yourself from within your own mind? Think about your favorite way or ways of limiting yourself or stopping yourself from being powerful in creating your whole life, including but not limited to the way you parent your children. What are your favorite "limiting beliefs"? What automatic reactions of carefulness did you learn and what events did you learn them from? How did you resolve to place limits on yourself to guard against repeating being hurt? When you get to the end of this chapter, come back to the beginning and see what you come up with about yourself in response to those questions.

The "Great Conversation," as Mortimer Adler called it in the introduction to the series "Great Books of the Western World," is the written record of the greatest thinkers of Western civilization. Adler and his colleagues at the University of Chicago in the 1940s compiled a list of 100 Great Books selected from the western canon of literature. We have, in the last half of the Twentieth Century, recognized as well the works of Eastern thinkers. The "Great Conversation" can now be said to refer to the whole conversation about what it is to be a human being. This conversation has been taking place since before recorded history, and the written record goes back a little over 5,000 years.

Human beings differ from all other species in that they can participate, through conversation with each other, in inventing who they are and how they live. As we talk about who we are and what it is to be a human being, we are both *discovering* the previous conversation to this point, and *inventing* right now what it is to be human. We are furthering the conversation both by discovering and inventing.

In reading this book you are engaging with me, and with all the thinkers I am indebted to, in order to continue the conversation, particularly about human power and about human love. Radical Parenting is really a conversation centered on these questions: What is human power and what is human love? How does one become powerful and loving? How does one empower other human beings and enable them to love?

I suggest that we begin with a tentative definition of power as the ability to get out of our own way. What follows explains what I mean by that.

THE BUILDING OF THE MIND IN CREATORS OF THE WORLD

I acknowledge primary recent contributions to this part of the Great Conversation by Ron Hubbard and Werner Erhard. I acknowledge the source of this conversation in Buddhism, Taoism, Yoga, and Vedantic Philosophy and in Western Philosophy, particularly Existentialism. This discussion addresses the following questions: What is a mind? What is a mind for? How does a mind get built? How does it work? How can you tame one and keep it from running away with you?

WHAT IS A MIND?

The model of the mind provided by Ron Hubbard includes this definition: *The mind is a linear arrangement of total multi-sensory recordings of successive moments of now.* The records are multisensory recordings, not just video and audio tapes but taste, touch, smell, balance, and feeling recordings as well. The stored records of the mind are linear in time from early to late in life. How long each of these "moments of now" recordings is varies. They can be as short as a few seconds or as long as a few hours. Moments are demarcated by noting some event, significant to you, that stands out. This begins the sequence of time called a "moment" and lasts until you consider the recording complete. Thousands and thousands of these moments are recorded, in a linear arrangement, from early in your life to recently in your life. The sum total of these stored recordings makes up the mind.

WHAT IS A MIND FOR?

A mind is for survival. We have minds in order to survive. Human beings, biologically, are a tube within a tube construction. We have a tube of skin covering up many more tubes inside us including our digestive system and our veins and arteries and capillaries. We became independent of the ocean way back there in evolution by creating our own ocean inside. We survive by putting water and food in one end of the tube and running it through us. Eventually it comes out tubes at the other end when we defecate and urinate, and little tubes that come to the surface of the skin where we sweat. If we are successful at this scarfing up of food and water, and we are able to get it done for us when we are too little to do it for ourselves, and we continue to do it long enough to survive to pubescence, we then put a male tube inside a female tube and make another tube. When we do this we have fulfilled our mission to survive and the mission of our species to survive. Basically it's a tube maintenance program.

The mind is for the survival of the being, so it must be of some use to scarf up things to put in the front end of the tube, and to find other tubes to play with long enough to create more tubes.

A more complete answer to the question "What is a mind for?" is: "A mind is for the survival of the being, or of anything the being considers itself to be." The problem is that the mind is what the being does its considering with! The mind gets to thinking that it *is* the being. The mind gets to thinking that its own survival is what it is for! And it can come to think that its own survival is more important than the survival of the being.

140

For example, Jack Benny, noted for his tightness with money, used to describe a scene in Central Park. A mugger would stick a gun in his ribs and say, "Your money or your life!" There would be dead silence. Then the mugger would repeat his demand. Jack would pause, then say, "I'm thinking! I'm thinking!" The difficulty he had choosing which was more important, his identification with his money or his identification with his life, illustrates the problem with having a mind. So did all those people who jumped out the windows on Wall Street when the stock market crashed in 1929.

Or, let's say you are sixteen years old and you were born in Baghdad and you want to be a good Moslem and a good citizen and a good follower of Saddam Hussein. You put on a uniform to preserve that identity and go with 80,000 of your brothers to Kuwait—and the Americans slaughter you and 60,000 others with the same identity within a few days. Your identification with your ideal cost you your life. A number of my friends and acquaintances got killed or maimed in Vietnam for the same reason.

Or, for another example, two phenomenological psychologists, named Schneideman and Farberow, wrote a book on suicide after almost seventeen years of research in which they studied 350 suicides. After interviewing friends and families, and studying the suicide notes left behind, they concluded that every suicide can be explained as "an attempt to maintain or enhance the self." The mind would rather be right and die than be wrong and live.

More and more teenagers are identifying more with their image than with their being. The internal judge who makes the assessments about life: "It's too hard," "I can't take it anymore," "It's not worth it," "Now, this will show them . . ." survives—at the cost of life itself.

The mind is a paranoid instrument and makes mistakes and cannot be trusted. In Eastern philosophy this is called the problem of ego.

Once the mind has decided that itself is what must survive, its survival comes from being right at any cost. A mind survives by being right and not wrong, by getting agreement and not disagreement from other minds. Its survival depends on being right and avoiding being wrong. This narcissistic preoccupation with itself, its own survival, necessitates defense of all of its assessments, judgments, decisions, stories, products and creations. The mind's identification with itself occurs as it is built as we grow up.

HOW DOES A MIND GET BUILT?

The "records of successive moments of now" can be divided into three types. All these successive moments of now can be envisioned as records stored on three spindles. Imagine three spindles for different kinds of records of the mind: Spindles A, B, and C. What are the criteria of selection for storage on one spindle as opposed to another?

Spindle A stores events involving a *threat to survival, pain, and a partial loss of consciousness.* These are called Class A events. An example of a Class A event is the following: Sally is four years old and is playing with her brother Tom, who is six. They are sailing a toy sailboat back and forth to each other in the shallow pond at a park near her house. Her mother is there, talking to a neighbor. It's a sunny day and the wind is blowing through the trees. Her dog, Rags, is there playing with others dogs and children. Suddenly, and without warning, her brother snatches up the boat, says "My boat!" and starts running away with it. Sally says, "No! It's my boat!" and starts to chase him. Rags notices the furor and joins in the chase. As they approach three concrete steps on the other side of the park, her brother runs down the steps, but just as Sally gets there Rags gets tangled up in her feet and she falls. She misses the steps but lands hard on her shoulder on the concrete sidewalk at the bottom. She scrapes her left arm and shoulder and bumps her head as she falls. The wind is knocked out of her. The next thing she knows, she is coming out of a fog, rolling over, trying to catch her breath, and she sees her mother running up and kneeling over her. The sunlight reflects off her mothers' glasses into her eyes, forcing her to squint. Her dog Rags is licking her face, and her brother Tom is saying "She's not hurt, She's not hurt!" in the background. She feels nauseous. Her mother scoops her up and carries her home, cleans her cuts, puts on Band-Aids and feeds her M&Ms. That's the end of the event. It is a Spindle A, Class A event, in which Sally experienced pain, a partial loss of consciousness and a threat to her survival, and she makes a total multi-sensory record at four years of age. The record may not remain conscious, it may become buried, it may be partially forgotten, it may be modified in conscious memory, but in some complete form, it remains.

Class B events on Spindle B are events that involve a *sudden, shocking loss with strong emotion, usually negative, and something important in the event is related to a previous Class A event.* For example, let's say the same little girl, Sally, is seven. She's running along a sidewalk behind her brother, next to the stadium. Her dog Rags is running behind her. Suddenly her brother cuts across the street. She follows. Rags follows her. There is a screech of brakes and a thud. Rags has been hit by a dump truck. She runs back. She bends down to look at Rags. She touches him. Her hand is sticky and she smells blood. She begins to cry. This is a Class B event—a sudden, shocking loss, with strong emotion, usually negative, associated with a previous Class A event. (Rags was running in the park, got tangled up in her feet and licked her face in the previously stored Class A event.)

Spindle C stores Class C records, which are anything at all associated with a Class A or Class B event. We have other experiences of trees, breezes, ponds, toy boats, parks, glasses, sunlight, sidewalks, brothers, wet sticky things, M & Ms, etc. and we make separate records of them, but we make records of the associations at the same time. We record experiences of events that are associated with Class A and B records and store the associated bodily experiences and memory with them.

By the time we are seven or eight years old, *everything in the world* is associated with a threat to our survival! This is why I say the mind, any mind, is essentially a paranoid instrument. We all have thousands of records in our memories of threats to our survival which we must avoid in the future in order to survive.

HOW DOES THE MIND WORK?

Here's how the associative mind works when we are adults. Let's say it's twelve years later and that same little girl Sally is now nineteen years old and a freshman at George Washington University. She goes to a park on a picnic with her boyfriend of several weeks, Gary. It's a sunny day and the wind is blowing through the trees. They've had some wine and cheese and a few bites of food when Sally leans back against a tree and Gary comes over to sit beside her. As he leans over to sit down beside her he squeezes her knee. "Ouch," she says. He replies, "You're not hurt, you're not hurt," and just as he bends over to kiss her *the sunlight glints off his glasses* right in her eyes. She kisses him back but feels nauseous and mildly anxious and slightly uncomfortable. She never goes out with him again. If you ask her why she quit dating him, Sally has all kinds of rational explanations: he's not her type; he doesn't have a good sense of humor; she doesn't want to be tied down right now, and so on. But these rational explanations have nothing to do with why she dropped him. She dropped him because her associative mind identified him with her forgotten Class A event from when she was four years old, including the pain, the nausea, and the threat to her survival. The memory of the event was triggered by the sunlight off his glasses and his voice saying, "You're not hurt."

But wait, let's take the same story and assume another associated outcome. Let's say the same events occur on the picnic. She leans back against the tree, he comes over to sit next to her and squeezes her knee, she says, "Ouch!" he says, "You're not hurt, you're not hurt." As he leans down to kiss her the sunlight glints off his glasses in her eyes, but this time when he kisses her, instead of nausea, she gets an insane urge for him to lick her face. As he pulls back, he does, at the end of a French kiss, accidentally, just barely lick the very edge of her lip. She marries him! If you ask her why she married him, Sally has all kinds of valid reasons: his family is wealthy; he's in med school; he came from a good family, and so on. But her associative mind chose him prior to all those rationalizations; she married him to bring her dog Rags back to life. (A lot of us married our dogs, at least the first time around!)

THE ILLUSION OF CONTROL

The rational, thinking, reflective mind thinks it is in control, but it isn't. Our rational decisions really aren't decisions at all, but rationalizations to justify the associations of the reactive mind. The reactive mind works according to associations. Control is an illusion provided by the quick-thinking (but not quite quick enough) reflective mind. The reflective mind just tags along closely behind the reaction and generates explanations in order to maintain the illusion of control.

If you think you know why you got married, or why you didn't, or why you got divorced, or picked a certain path in life, or got married again, or had children, or moved, you are seriously deluded. Your belief that you are in control is a complete illusion.

I'm not asking you to believe this instead of whatever you already believe. Instead, I ask that you use it as a temporary model: imagine it to be true, for the time being, and try it on for size. This has important implications for how you might raise your child.

If we make this temporarily true as an experiment for just a moment, one thing is quite obvious; all the beliefs you have defended were merely for the sake of providing you with an illusion of control. All the theories you have expounded explaining your motivation for doing thus and such are all bullshit. The truth is you're not in control at all, and all your attempts to fool other people only show who was really fooled all along—you!

NOTICING YOUR NOTICING

Now hold that view for a moment and let me present you with another idea. You are now looking at ink on a page. The light reflects off of the page and print and goes to your eye, through the lens to the back of the eyeball, and there a certain chemical reaction is triggered. This reaction throws off an electron, which causes another chemical reaction, which throws off an electron, and there is an electrical transmission up the optic nerve to the visual cortex. There, in the visual cortex, a chemical reaction occurs, and you see the words. The place where you are creating seeing the words is in your brain. That is, the creation of the sight of the words takes place in your brain at that very millisecond the last chemical reaction occurs. Where the words are in your experience are on the page, outside of your brain. You are creating the words in your brain and experiencing them as outside of you. You create the world in your brain by a chemical reaction, but where you consider the world to be, is outside of you. You are also creating the room you're in or whatever surrounding you have around you, all the other people in your life, and everything in view of you at any given time.

You do the same thing with sound. Someone make noises with their voice box, the vibrations reach the little hammer, anvil and drum in your inner ear, a chemical reaction occurs, causing an electro-chemical transmission to your brain—and you hear. You integrate the sight and sound and other sense data, and you also make meaning out of the words. This is all completely effortless. It requires no strain or effort or trying on your part. It happens automatically simply because you exist as the perceptual organizing machine you are. It is the most magnificent thing you will ever do, yet you give yourself no special credit for it. It doesn't count because everyone else does it too—it doesn't make you special in any comparative way. It is not important to who you think you are, yet it is ongoingly, millisecond by millisecond, the most magnificent thing you will ever do! Nothing you ever achieve with your mind or your life will come close to matching the miracle of the creation of the world by your involuntary nervous system, effortlessly, just by being here. We all know that this accomplishment doesn't really count. What counts, we are convinced, is all the bullshit having to do with our performance and our products.

PUTTING IT ALL TOGETHER

I want you to consider two ideas at once now. You are the creator of the world and you have no control. You are out of control. Control is purely an illusion of your reflective mind, to protect you from discerning that you are helplessly at the beck and call of your reactive mind. Yet, at the same time, as a being, you are the creator of the world. And when you die, for all practical purposes, the world comes to an end. Just consider both of those things true at the same time.

There is a story told about all the Greek gods sitting around on Mount Olympus. They were all-knowing and all-seeing. They knew all the whole past and the whole future. So, very soon, they became bored. In order to entertain themselves and pass the time they started inventing and playing games. One of their favorite games was one called, "Let's pretend that what is not here is more important than what is here." This game, pretending that what is not here is more important than what is here, became the common obsession, and they played and played, until after a while, they forgot it was a game. They forgot it was a game for a long time, in fact until right now. It's my job now to remind you. So, I am reminding you: It's just a game. The idea that something that is not here is more important than what is here is just a game! It was just pretend. It was just a pretense. It was just something you got in your mind as you grew up and it is not real. In helping your child develop a mind, this could turn out to be an important idea! We human beings, because we have minds, forget that playing toward the future is just a game and that our fundamental identity as creators of the world, in the moment, in the flow of creation, is reality. When we modify the modification, or as the yogis say, when we inhibit the modifications of the mind, we discover what is there other than mind. And what is there is the creator of the world, you, the one who effortlessly makes the whole world happen.

I am not talking about something new in history, just something relatively new in Western history. Yoga, which means yoke—that which connects together intellect and spirit, or being and mind—is primarily concerned with exactly the topic we are now considering.

THE WISDOM OF YOGA

In the millennia-old philosophy and practice of yoga, as summarized in the Yoga Sutras of Patanjali, countering the mind's distortions is given the highest priority. After yoga had been around for a few thousand years, a yoga teacher and scholar named Patanjali wrote the *Yoga Sutras*. By the time he wrote the *Yoga Sutras,* many different methods for the practice of yoga had been developed: Karma Yoga, Bhakti Yoga, Tantric Yoga, Kundalini Yoga, Hatha Yoga and so on. These yogas of service, love, sex, work, physical health, and the philosophy of yoga had all undergone literally thousands of years of development.

The "Sutra" form in Sanskrit is a stylized form embodying all there is to be known about any area of study into one hundred sutras, or verses. These are short phrases, limited to about a two-line statement, organized in the specific form of a sequence of one hundred statements. The most comprehensive sutras come first. The first sutra says what subsequent sutras are about. For example, if we were to put the whole body of knowledge we call physics into one hundred statements, the first statement would be, "These are the sutras of Physics, which is the study of matter in the physical universe." Then we would have ninety-nine statements left to cover all of physics.

The second sutra is designated as the most comprehensive overview of the whole of the work and practices of the area under consideration.

In our example, we would be expected, in the second sutra, to say in one statement what all of physics is about.

The second sutra of the *Yoga Sutras,* the one that most comprehensively covers the subject of all the different practices of yoga, is this: "The objective of all Yoga is to bring about an inhibition of the modifications of the mind."

The modifications of the mind are memories, principles, conclusions, morals, imaginings and beliefs. We might say, giving our explication of the reactive mind and the reflective mind, that: "The objective of all Yoga is to bring about the inhibition of the modifications of the minds." The "minds" are the reactive mind and the reflective mind. The reactive mind simply associates the stored memories we discussed at the beginning of this chapter. The reflective mind is the rationalizer who makes up good reasons to justify the associations of the reactive mind. The objective of all of the practices of yoga, according to Patanjali, is to bring about the inhibition of those minds, *because that is what allows us to discover our true identity as beings who create the world.*

IN CONCLUSION

These minds we have are the smoke and mirrors that keep us from attending to the reality of being. Assuming that the reactive mind truly determines how we live and what we do, and that the reflective mind preserves the illusion of control through explanation and interpretation, and that the fundamental identity of ourselves as human beings is as creators of the world, then how can a person be consciously in control of his life?

These presumptions make an immense difference in our attitudes toward our children and the task of parenting. First, we may as well just give up the illusion of control. Second, we can know that we are, from the beginning, already sufficiently taken care of by our involuntary nervous systems. Third, we are going to have minds; we inevitably grow minds and they are of some use, but to value our minds as our primary identity is a big mistake. Fourth, if we identify with being, that is, consider ourselves as well as our children as *beings who notice,* we might become *conscious creators, using the reactive and reflective minds instead of being used by them.*

But how in the hell can you do all that? I think the best way to start is with your view of yourself. You are a being who has a mind. The being you are possesses the mind you have. Then it is easy to view yourself and your child as equal with regard to being, although your baby may be a little superior to you with regard to noticing. If you identify with the being you are, who notices, rather than with the mind you are, who thinks, it changes everything. Instead of keeping your mind in charge of your being, you can switch them, and put your being in charge of your mind.

This raises a bunch of questions. How do you do that? Even more important, how do you raise your children in such a way that they can escape being victimized by their own minds? If your children learn to be identified with their being and using their minds, rather than being used by their minds, they will learn it from you, their primary role model. *The best way for you to learn what it is you have to teach is by learning from them when they are young and growing,* and then not training them out of the wisdom they already had when they were born. That's what this next chapter is about.

15 ⚬⚭ THE DEVELOPMENTAL CONTINUUM OF LEARNING: A SUMMARY AND SYNTHESIS OF THE WORK OF JEAN PIAGET AND ERIK ERIKSON ON THE GROWTH OF THE MIND AND PERSONALITY

THE GROWTH AND DEVELOPMENT OF the mind and the personality needs to be studied in detail to appreciate how we fulfill our human destiny. Human beings are uniquely adapted to life by having developed extreme intelligence. Learning the enormous amount of information needed to survive is primarily done during childhood. Most childhood learning—walking, talking, eating, and countless other small and large physical, mental and cultural skills—occurs by the child observing and imitating others and experimenting with gravity. With the exception of language, hardly any of the most valuable things learned are cognitive, or involve thinking, or use of the brain's frontal lobes in any way. Even the learning of language, and eventually abstract cognitive ability, must be based on the experiential learning that precedes it.

Jean Piaget and others have outlined a model of the growth of a child's mind through stages of development. The end result of cognitive development in Piaget's model, abstract cognitive ability, is the ability to think as most of us think of thinking. This doesn't take place until around ten or eleven years of age. But because, in our culture, we are inordinately interested in, and dependent on, one way of transmitting information—verbally—and one kind of information—abstract ideas—we are constantly forcing abstract ideas on children who do not have the developed capacity to get them. Most of us believe that once a child has learned to talk they can generalize and reason like an adult. This is a major mistake.

The following is an extrapolation from Piaget's pool table experiment, which he designed after years of carefully keeping daily journals of the intellectual growth of his own and other children. He designed the experiment to see if what he observed in those limited instances was generalizable to all children.

Let's say we have a billiards table (like a pool table but with no pockets), one cue ball, one object ball to shoot at, and one pool cue. We bring in a bunch of four- and five-year-olds, one at a time, and show them how to use the cue to hit the cue ball toward a bank on the table so that it bounces off and hits the object ball. They have a lot of fun shooting the ball into the bank and now and then it accidentally hits the object ball. We then replace the cue ball and object ball on the same spots and the child plays at hitting the bank some more. He or she never goes beyond shooting at random.

Now we bring in six- and seven-year-olds. They shoot at random for a while and then get better at hitting the object ball with the cue ball on almost every shot, as long as both are replaced at the same spots. They have found a spot on the bank that works, and they keep hitting it and making the cue ball hit the object ball. However, if we move the location of the object ball they start out at random again, until they find the spot they need to hit to bank the cue ball to the location of the new object ball. If we move the object ball again, they start out at random again to find the one spot on the bank that allows them to hit the object ball. They can do this "finding a spot that works" exercise repeatedly, without generalizing the skill to significantly decrease the number of random trials it takes to find the new spot on the bank that corresponds to the changed location of the object ball.

When we bring in the eight- and nine-year-olds, they will, after a short time, find the spot on the bank that allows them to hit the object ball every time. When we move the object ball up or down the table, they will, in a lesser number of attempts and not at random, find a spot on the bank, up or down the table, that allows them to hit the object ball again. If we move the ball to the left, they will begin immediately to hit the cue ball to the left of the prior spot on the bank, and quickly find the correct angle. If we ask them, "How did you do that? How did you know where to shoot on the bank to hit the object ball when we move it?" they can't answer the question. They are unable to articulate the general principle on the basis of which they are operating.

When we bring in ten- and eleven-year-olds, they will do as the eight- and nine-year-olds did. But in addition to that skill they will demonstrate the additional skill of giving some kind of verbal explanation that *the ball leaves the bank at the same angle it hits the bank.* The ten- and eleven-year-olds have attained *abstract cognitive ability.* The four- and five-year-olds were at the level of *concrete operations* (they could hit the cue ball with the stick) and the other subsets by age were at stages of development between concrete operations and abstract cognitive ability.

Now that we have that picture about how children develop cognitive skills over time, let's talk about some of the work of Erik Erikson, and psychosocial development.

Erik Erikson came up with a theory of human development based on a universal set of problems to be faced at certain ages for all human beings. These stages of growth are universal and independent of culture, though the way they are handled varies from culture to culture. He said that at each one of the stages of human development (or "passages" as Gail Sheehy calls them) certain conflicts must be resolved in order for the person to proceed to the next stage.

These are not abstract cognitive states, they are more like "feeling states" in which experiential conclusions are being reached by the developing child. The conclusions are reached through resolving a dialectical conflict that is a result of remembering and compiling experiences in some way that is not quite like abstract thinking. For example, in the first stage of life from birth to one year of age, Erikson says the conflict is "Trust versus Mistrust" and must be resolved on the side of trust in order for development to continue. The infant must "make up her mind," so to speak, based on her experience of being here, about whether this place outside the womb is a place she can trust or not. Those who resolve on the side of "Trust" go on to the next stage of growth and face the next conflict. Those who resolve on the side of distrust don't develop anymore and die or remain institutionalized. Erikson and others cite evidence from institutionalized babies who have a higher death rate from what has been called marasmus or "hospitalism." These babies get changed and fed but not played with much, and about thirty percent more of them die in the first year of life than the norm for fed and changed babies who are touched, held and played with regularly. (Perhaps because limbic neural development is inadequate!)

Once the child has resolved the conflict on the side of trust, he then moves on to the next stage, which lasts through years two and three and is called "Autonomy versus Shame." Here the child either "gets" that it's okay to have and use his energy to run around, get control of his sphincter valves, and jump and play and make noise, or he becomes chronically ashamed of moving, investigating, peeing or defecating, or having energy. A certain number of us peel off at this point and the rest go on to the next stage.

At age four to six, the conflict is called "Initiative versus Guilt," and at the "school age" from six to twelve or so, the conflict is called "Competence versus Incompetence." It's here, at these stages, that a life of creativity and self-responsibility is either nurtured or squelched. What happens during these years generates a lot of the complaints that people in psychotherapy voice about how they were raised. Their most common complaints are about the methods of control imposed upon them by parents and teachers to "get them on the right track." The most often-used method of control is to shame them into obedience and to threaten them with punishment.

Children made to feel guilty are more easily controlled but never mature beyond performance consciousness. Even if they conclude that it is okay to have initiative, they can get stuck in worrying about their own adequacy and competence when judged by teachers and peers. Unless initiative is supported and the child concludes that it is okay to initiate investigations and make mistakes, and continues to do so, his growth is over. (This group is where most Republicans and education majors come from.)

INTEGRATING THE THEORIES OF ERIK ERIKSON AND JEAN PIAGET

Now let's go back to Piaget for a moment and relate his stages of cognitive development to Erikson's stages of psychosocial development. During "the school age"—Erikson's "Competence versus Incompetence"—the growing child completes his intellectual development to the highest stage in Piaget's model (abstract cognitive ability). He can then abstract from experience and create generalizations that apply to a variety of circumstances. By about eleven we are all blooming experts. We can also make generalizations about judgments that are themselves generalizations, both our own and others'. Having attained this skill, we then begin to generalize about who we are. This is what the next crisis is about. The crisis of adolescence is called "Identity versus Role Diffusion." This is really the first life-conflict we face after having developed abstract cognitive ability. This is the conflict beyond which a large percentage of our current population doesn't grow. This conflict during the adolescent years, and the next one which happens during young adulthood and is called "Intimacy vs. Isolation," pretty much cover the gamut of what most people see psychotherapists for, up until age fifty or so.

In our culture, we have an alarming suicide rate for people aged fourteen to twenty-four. Various theories have been postulated by experts, about how the culture's breaking down, or that our kids have too many options to choose from, or that the lack of family values is responsible. These theories all seem to have some merit. But for me, *the biggest problem with establishing identity is the problem of identifying with the mind to the exclusion of the body.* After being taught that your performance is all that counts all your life, it is easy to come to think that your performance is who you are. The being in the body, the fundamental organism for experiencing the world, becomes irrelevant. What counts is how well you think other people will think you are doing.

I believe that teenagers who identify themselves with their minds, who consider themselves to be their minds, live or die by their judgments. In order to be right, some of them kill themselves. In order to defend their conclusions they are willing to die. They kill themselves to maintain their identity. If you consider who you are to be your mind, the way you survive is by being right. If you have to kill the being in which the mind resides in order to be right, no problem, that's not really who you are. All those suicides are cases of mistaken identity.

The same kind of mistaken identity is what causes young men to put on uniforms and go to war to be "good Americans" or "good Muslims" or "good Nazis" or "good" whatever identity they happened to be dumped into.

The last stage in Erikson's paradigm I will mention here, "Intimacy versus Isolation," has to do with the ability to share your life out loud with others. For more on that and on the last stages of life, read Erikson's *Childhood and Society* (Norton, 1993) or Gail Sheehy's *Passages* (Bantam, 1984) or *New Passages* (Ballentine, 1996) or my chapter in *Radical Honesty,* "Telling the Truth in a Couple" which is an explication and synthesis of some of the work of Erikson, Martin Buber, Abraham Maslow and Erich Fromm.

Developing your own capacity for intimacy is critical to being a good parent, so I recommend radical honesty as a learning tool for anyone who had children before they themselves grew up (which is what happens to damn near all of us, because we live in an adolescent culture).

PARENTING TO SUPPORT PSYCHO-SOCIAL AND COGNITIVE DEVELOPMENT

Using Piaget's and Erikson's models, what can we infer about parenting? Well, first, they should be a big relief for parents. They suggest that one good way to look at the whole job of parenting is to see it as just nurturing natural development from birth to adulthood. Maybe if we just be alert and let things unfold, that's enough. Maybe the job isn't as complicated as we think. Maybe if we bond with children one at a time, love them and keep an eye out, that's good enough. So we just touch them a lot and play with them, and hand them around a lot in the first year, to help them establish trust. Then we keep watching as they teach themselves to crawl and walk and toilet train, and keep modern dangerous things like live wires out of their way while they do it. Then look and listen and admire and delight in all they create while growing a mind, and don't expect them to understand fairness, God, general principles of good and evil, and other abstract cognitive things too early. Play a lot of physical games with them to develop their bodily skills and love of physical action. Then, be there with the relevant information when their minds can get it, and with opportunities for them to stay in their experience in their bodies when their bodies change. When they are sixteen or so, we're mostly done. Maybe, after all is said and done, we can say to each other, "Now that wasn't so bad, was it?"

I really think it's just about that simple, but just because it's simple doesn't mean it's not hard. The kind of parent it would take to do this is fundamentally a whole person, centered in the experience of being, using her mind in service to her being, to act with care, after noticing what is required in the moment. An enlightened parent raises enlightened children. Cool parents have cool children.

Children learn from what their parents do, and from how they are, and from how they "be" in the world. What the parents say is not very important at all, particularly if their way of being contradicts what they say. Parents who have forgiven their own parents don't teach their children to blame. Victims raise victims. People who have grown from victim to creator by working through their grudges and idealizations of their own parents and teachers become creators rather than victims. Creators raise creators.

Most parents are not cool. Most parents have some kind of axe to grind, and haven't yet recovered from their own childhoods. Most parents are damaged goods because of not having yet recovered from how they were parented.

People who have learned forgiveness are forgiving, and people who haven't aren't. I have harped on this a lot, but bear with me. If you can forgive your parents you can forgive almost anyone, including your mate and your own children. In my experience, some of the "nicest," most decent, most ideal-appearing parents were often the most poisonous to their children, and hardest to forgive. Particularly if you had parents who were overly concerned about appearances, about "manners" and about "being polite," it will probably take some serious work to get over being mad at them. Remember that, and interrupt yourself when you start teaching that politeness bullshit to your own kids, trying to "make them behave." If you can keep from being like "the church lady" Dana Carvey plays on Saturday Night Live, you can save your own kids a lot of trouble and let them grow up to adulthood instead of staying stuck in adolescence until they are fifty or sixty years old. It takes a lot of hard psychological work to forgive your parents and let bygones be bygones. Make it easier on your own kids. What we all have to do to grow up is:

(1) Understand and undo how we were poisoned by conditional love, or some other manner of abuse done in the name of "helping" or "educating" us;

(2) Get angry at those who so poisoned us, and experience the anger, and then get over it;

(3) Grieve for our lost love, and the specialness we felt with them that was lost as we grew up to take care of ourselves;

(4) Forgive them without trying to change their behavior, and whether they apologize or not, and whether they deny our memory of events or not. Then finally, we get to

(5) Parent our own children with love and gratitude, as we feel the same for our own parents.

Then, after all, you can say to your parents the same thing you can say to your kids, and the same thing your kids can say to you and to their kids: "Now that wasn't so bad, was it?"

The next chapter gives you exercises that enhance your own ability to identify with the being you are as primary, and the mind you have as secondary, so that you can begin the process of healing yourself and your source family and, with them, pass on that wisdom to your children.

16 ❧ DEVELOPING SKILLFULNESS IN NOTICING

BRINGING ABOUT THE INHIBITION OF the modifications of the minds is the key to Radical Parenting. In order to inhibit the modifications of the reactive and reflective minds, your own minds, you have to distinguish between noticing and thinking. Noticing, or what has been called the Awareness Continuum, can be arbitrarily divided into three parts:

(1) You can notice what is going on inside the confines of your own skin, right now.
(2) You can notice what is going on outside of you in the world right now.
(3) You can notice what is going through your mind right now.

That's all. There ain't no more. That's it, that's all you can notice: Inside, Outside, Upside Down (that is also the title of a great children's book by Berenstain).

We're now going to do an exercise that focuses on noticing what is going on outside of your body right now, in order to distinguish between noticing and thinking. The exercise is called, "It's obvious and I imagine." You can do this with your mate as well as with your kids.

Two people sit opposite each other and take turns saying what they notice about the other person and then what they imagine. *Noticing* is constrained to what is observable about the other person at the very moment of speaking, in the here and now. *Imagining* is completely free. The idea is to sort out "referent words," or *words that point* to something extant in the here and now, from words that attribute meaning to what is in front of you.

In this exercise, the dumber you are the better. One person says, "I notice you have on a blue shirt. I imagine you bought it at Sears." Then it's the other person's turn. "I notice you have on a watch. I imagine you are concerned about time." The noticing or the observation is descriptive of something that is actually there. The imaginings can be as fanciful as you like. "It's obvious you have eyes. I imagine you are crazy," still meets the rules of the game, even though the association between the observation and the imagining is not clear. The focus of doing the exercise is on developing the ability to know the difference between the real world and the world of interpretation.

If you are co-parenting, sit down opposite your mate when the child is asleep, or being taken care of by someone else. If it's not handy to do that, ask someone you know to do the exercise with you. Sit with your chairs facing each other. The first person says, "I notice you _____," and state in the blank space something you notice about the person across from you. This is something anyone could notice, something simple, like "I notice you have on a shirt." Next you say "and I imagine _____" and say anything at all that you imagine about that person. It may be related to the observation in some easily identifiable way, or it may not. Imaginings are completely free, it's noticings that are completely limited, and what they are limited to is the here and now of the moment of speaking. Noticings are observations, limited to the here and now. Imaginings are completely unrestrained. Then the second person says what they notice and what they imagine. Keep going back and forth. This becomes, if you stick with it, a meditation. If you continue this exercise beyond the state of boredom, as I have with trainees in gestalt therapy over the years, you eventually enter into an altered state of consciousness. You wake up—like sometimes happens in sitting meditation.

After a while, both of you close your eyes and visualize your partner. Describe your partner while both of you have your eyes closed, and then have your partner describe you. Open your eyes after that and discuss how well you were able to give detailed descriptions of each other when you had been paying attention. Talk. Clearly point out to each other the distinction between imagining and noticing. (If you would like a video tape demonstrating this exercise as well as some other points made in this chapter you can call 1 800 EL TRUTH and order one from us.)

SUMMARY OF EXERCISE ONE

There are three things a person can notice: Inside (the body), Outside (the environment) and upside down (the mind). We are all in the habit of mistaking what we interpret as reality for reality itself. We often operate as though our imaginings were the same thing as reality. When you see something that is not real, or hear something that is not real, it's called a hallucination. However, often when you think something that is not real, it passes for normal, although it's just as crazy as other auditory and visual hallucinations. This common mistake is trained into us. We have been taught to lie about reality, by asserting that our assumptions about "how it is" or "how it should be," or the meaning we make about reality, is reality itself.

The *observable world* can be distinguished from the *world of interpretation* and it is valuable to do so. If I ask you what you notice about me and you report an interpretation as though it were an observation, or I ask you what you notice in your body and you give me some explanation about what you are feeling or why, that is what "bullshit" is. To do a halfway good job of partnering and parenting you have to get beyond just bullshitting each other. Most people don't.

When we develop our skills in listening and watching each other in a couple, or with our child, and we practice making distinctions between what we observe about others and what we imagine, we become clearer in our communications with each other.

The point of this is not to make imagining taboo, or judge that there is anything wrong with imagining. Imaginings are fine and imagination is a wonderful thing. "Let's pretend" is a really fun game to play with kids, particularly from about four to seven years of age. Those years are just wonderful for both the parent and the child, filled with delight and happiness and fun. Play as much as you can and invent and imagine to your heart's content. It is an absolutely wonderful thing and an important skill to expand and make the most of. Developing the ability to imagine is vital to play.

While we develop the precious ability to imagine, however, it helps to know the difference between fantasy and reality. Point it out casually to children and don't harp on it. Knowing the difference between a fantasy and what is real becomes increasingly important as we grow older.

During adolescence we often begin not only pretending, but pretending that we are not pretending at the same time. That gets us in a lot of trouble, not only during adolescence but throughout adulthood. I have written several books about this kind of trouble. One value of imagining is that, especially if you are good at distinguishing between imagining and reality, you can sometimes make real something that was once only an imagining. You can make future dreams come true if you know the difference between them and current reality.

FURTHER EXERCISES TO DISTINGUISH BETWEEN NOTICING AND THINKING

EXERCISE 2: HOT SEAT WORK

The following is from the introduction to Gestalt Therapy "hot seat" work I use in my work with groups. It has in it some valuable verbal clues about how to distinguish noticing from thinking, observing from imagining. If you participate in a Radical Parenting workshop you will get an opportunity to observe and participate in hot seat work. Usually we sit on chairs in a big circle and the seat next to me is kept empty. Whomever wants to respond to the following invitation can come up and sit next to me and everyone can watch us work together. The introduction to the hot seat can be understood as instruction on how to speak and listen honestly, and to help each other discover the truth in the course of a shared conversation.

Here's what I tell people:

This empty chair is called the "hot seat." It's called the hot seat because when you sit in it, everyone in the room is looking at you and listening to you and watching you carefully. I'll be listening with my eyes as well as my ears. Every sound that comes out of you, every gesture you make, every move, will be considered a communication. When you come up here you are taking responsibility for requesting our focus in order to seek help in undoing some of your beliefs that don't work anymore, but you are still attached to—things that may have helped you survive when you were younger, or in other circumstances, but that don't work for you anymore.

You may be nervous when you come up here. That is normal. If you were not nervous at all, that would actually be more worrisome. When I look and listen to you I am looking for accord, for things seeming to fit together and make sense, for a unitary "gestalt," a consistency of words, sounds, gestures and actions—a way they all seem to go together. I will also be looking for inconsistency, for apparent contradictions of flow, or form or content. Where we find disunity we will then seek to maximize the disunity, break up the contradictory messages, break down the way they are held together, so that a new unity can be attained.

While you are in the hot seat and while you are in the group, I would like you to help me enforce three taboos. The first taboo is against any "why . . . because" games. We do this BECAUSE (and you notice we are playing a "why . . . because" game now, while I explain why we taboo "whys" and "becauses" during hot seat work) we don't want to be led into the mind; we want to be led away from the mind and toward experience. So we substitute "how" for "why," and the word "and" for "because." So if you start off saying, "I am mad at you because . . ." you go into your mind to present the reasons for why your anger is justified. When you say, "How I am angry is that my heart is beating fast, my breath is rapid and short, I feel heat in my face and chest and arms, and I am imagining hitting you and think-ing of things to say to hurt you and make you mad like, 'You're an idiot!'" Your attention is directed to how you are the source of your own anger by your attachment to standards the other person should live up to. When you experience how you are angry rather than run off into why you are angry, you have a chance of gettting over it.

The second taboo is against using the word "it." The word "it" is a way of attributing power and responsibility that rightfully belongs to you to some abstract outside source. I'll ask you to substitute the word "I" for it. So instead of saying "it" makes me mad, you say "I" make me mad. Then you can focus on how you make yourself mad through your attachment to how the other person or people "should" behave. (It is your attachment to how they should behave that is the source of your anger. This is absolutely critical to get in relation to your chil-dren, especially when they become teenagers.)

The third taboo is against using the word "but" because "but" is a way of saying one thing and then setting it aside and saying some-thing contrary to what you just said, or at odds with what you just said. For example, if I say, "I love you but your feet stink" the word "but" separates the assertion "I love you" from the assertion "your feet stink." This linguistic setting aside of apparent contradiction is handled by using "and" in the place of "but." So when you say, "I love you and your feet stink" both assertions remain equal and must vie for dominance, one over the other, rather than kept separate linguistically to avoid the conflict. So the three taboos are: No "why . . . because" games, no "its" and no "buts." Okay, the hot seat is available.

If you want to do this as an exercise in a couple, go ahead and give it a shot. You will probably be surprised at how often you use these linguistic habits to control or protect, or make sure things get interpreted correctly.

EXERCISE 3: WORD FAST

Make an explicit agreement with your partner or a friend to spend a day together, or a whole weekend, without speaking. You interact just as you usually do, except you don't talk to each other. You can gesture, write short notes if necessary, and act out charades if you have something really complicated to communicate.

What usually happens in this exercise is that people who have begun to start taking each other for granted start noticing each other. After your kids are a little older, include them in on the game. Set a specific time that the word fast ends, and then everybody can talk about what happened when they were not speaking. This is one of the simplest possible things to do, yet it has profound impact, and it is often one of the most hilariously funny learning experiences a family or couple can have together.

EXERCISE 4: SHOULDS

"Shoulds" are another way we trick ourselves into believing that we are in control. We all have a church lady inside telling us what we "should" and "shouldn't" do. This exercise is to own how hard we are on ourselves with our internal judge and to have an experience of letting up on ourselves.

Partner up with someone and sit opposite from them in a chair. Then decide who is A and who is B.

Part 1: Partner A tells Partner B a whole bunch of things A thinks she "should" do, and things she thinks she "shouldn't" do. For example, "I should wash the dishes" or "I shouldn't take so long to get ready in the mornings." After each should or shouldn't, Partner B responds, in a good, loud voice, "NO!" Switch sides after about 4 minutes: B then lists his shoulds, one at a time, and A says "NO!"

Part 2: This time partner B repeats back to Partner A all of A's shoulds and shouldn'ts. Partner A strongly and expressively resists by saying "NO!" to each should and shouldn't. Three minutes each side. If the "should-er" can't remember all of his partner's shoulds, he can just make up some of his own.

Part 3: Talk to each other about what this exercise brought up for you.

Part 4: If you have done this exercise with a group of friends, after the pairings, form a circle again and have a group discussion of the exercise.

Some general comments: You will notice that some of your shoulds and shouldn'ts are more important to you than others. The point of the exercise is that they are all imaginary and distinguishable from reality. We are trying to distinguish between the observable and imagined worlds. All shoulds are illusions. They live in the imagined world. All shoulds are illusory, especially your most precious ones. Shouldism is next to sadism. We often treat our shoulds as if they existed in reality. They do not. You can't point to a should. They don't exist in the real world. When we believe in the reality of our shoulds, we have been driven crazy. If insanity is seeing or hearing or believing things that simply are not there, believing too strongly in shoulds is a particular form of insanity.

Part 5: Close your eyes and imagine, that just for the moment, there is absolutely nothing you should do or shouldn't do. Notice what that feels like in your body. Notice what happens in your mind. What would your world be like without any shoulds? What is left if you don't have any shoulds? What are you left with when you simply suspend all shoulds?

If you don't have obligations to help you avoid facing the reality of your life, you must then discover what you prefer to do, what you want to do, what you consider worth doing and feel called forth to do. Once you no longer live in the jail of obligation, you are left to discover your bliss. Instead of being pushed by shoulds, you can follow your bliss. Instead of following out of obligation, you lead according to your bliss. After getting this, the ongoing challenge is to notice when you turn your preference into a should. This often happens rather quickly with those of us who have been so well trained in shoulds we haven't paused to notice what we actually want to do.

There is something relieving and fun and at the same time scary about the lack of shoulds and shouldn'ts. Shoulds and shouldn'ts are beliefs that keep you at a lower level of consciousness. Shoulds and shouldn'ts are the mind's attempt to control your life. If you want to learn how to use the "shouldistic" nature of the mind, rather than have it use you, you must gain a perspective that transcends your shoulds.

This is the primary value of transcendence: To decrease the power of the imaginary life of our shouldistic minds in order to be centered in the experience of the here and now. Only then can we use our imaginations to create our lives from envisioning the future we prefer, rather than the unconsciously learned obligations from the past.

It is for this reason that systematic practices that involve noticing are critical. If we develop skillfulness in noticing, and keep it sharp through regular practice, we find that the instructions for how to be a halfway decent parent are in the glove compartment. In the vehicle we are riding around in, the glove compartment is called the limbic brain.

Step V

Raising Creators Is Easy,
Given That Children Already Are Creators

17 ⚏ LEARNING TO TOLERATE JOY

SOME OF US HAVE WORKED through anger and shame and sexual taboos in the course of growing beyond just growing up. We were surprised at what came next. We were surprised to discover that we are more afraid of joy than we are of any of the other emotions. The joy and celebration of freedom that emerges when we get free from most of the mind's taboos is so unfamiliar it is almost too much to bear.

Many of us have this built-in mechanism to guard against being overwhelmed by love—being unmanned and unwomanned and undone from our identity as survivors. Here is how the mechanism works: We fall in love and feel love for another person. For a little while it is just wonderful—more wonderful than we can allow ourselves to experience—so our minds, whose duty it is to make sure we are not overwhelmed by any experience, save us from that experience of love by associating the current experience of love with earlier records of having *lost* this same kind of love. We close down the love with anxiety—to prevent the intensity.

We experience love and immediately turn it into nostalgia for lost love because we cannot bear letting love come and go. We have lost it before, our minds say, and it was terrible, so don't do that again. Our mothers and fathers and teachers and other big people loved us conditionally and we never quite got the conditions met. We lost their love and thought it was our fault for not being careful enough. We didn't stay in control. This time we will be careful. We will stay in control. We are so careful we block the feeling with the memory of the loss of the feeling.

Love becomes blocked by mourned lost love and romanticized nostalgia in order to satisfy the mind's need to preserve the illusion of control. It is our mind's job to protect us. We think that who we are is our mind. Our parents and teachers taught us that who we are is our minds. Ignoring our limbic brain and believing that the function of our neocortex is to control our reptilian brain, they have taught us to be on guard against surrender. They were dead wrong. Who we actually are, our real identity, is as *beings, in love.*

We already knew this when we were little, but we didn't know we knew it. In the course of growing up, we got trained out of it by people who thought that developing our minds and identifying with them was more important than staying aware of the experience in our bodies and the warmth of contact with other people. Once we get this again, and get that we have always known this in our bones, life changes from making-do-the-the-best-we-can (survival) to making out pretty happily in the world.

SWEET LAND OF LIBERTY

I quote now from the brilliant book written by my friend Grace Llewellyn, a book written directly to kids, to help them make up their minds about staying in school or not. I love Grace and I love her book *The Teenage Liberation Handbook,* which has become a classic for homeschoolers and unschoolers everywhere. It helps when you read the section of her book reproduced here, to remember the work of Stanley Milgram about Adolph Eichmann which we reviewed in chapter twelve of this book. Here's what Grace says:

"'The most potent weapon in the hands of the oppressor is the mind of the oppressed.' Steven Biko

"How strange and self-defeating that a supposedly free country should train its young for a life of totalitarianism."

"No, David, wait until after class to use the bathroom."

"Unfortunately, your daughter would rather entertain the class than participate appropriately."

"Good morning, class. Please open your textbooks to page thirty. Thank you, John, you need to open your book to page thirty."

"Carter, if I have to ask you again to sit down, you'll be taking a trip to the office."

"Miguel, you are not in math. Please put it away. Remember, fifteen percent of your grade in my class comes from participation and attitude."

"Ladies! Gentlemen! Let's keep the noise down in the halls."

"I'd love to hear what you have to say, Monty, but you will have to raise your hand first."

"Tonight you need to finish the exercises on page 193 and read the next section."

"Marisa, I need a written explanation as to why you didn't turn in your homework today."

"Laura, put away the book. If I catch you again it's a zero for the day, and that's not something you can afford."

"What do you think of when you hear the word freedom? The

end of slavery? The end of the Berlin wall? A prisoner tunneling his way out of solitary confinement in Chile with a spoon? An old woman escaping her broken body in death? Gorillas dancing in the jungle instead of sulking behind bars? When I hear the word freedom I remember the sweetest sunlight pouring over my teenaged cheeks on the first sleeping-in mornings of summer vacations.

"Do you go to school? Yes? Then—

"You are not free.

"The most overwhelming reality of school is CONTROL. School controls the way you spend your time (what is life made of if not time?), how you behave, what you read, and to a large extent what you think. In school you can't control your own life. Outside of school you can, at least to the extent that your parents trust you to. 'Comparing me to those who are conventionally schooled,' writes twelve-year-old unschooler Colin Roch, 'Is like comparing the freedoms of a wild stallion to those of cattle in a feedlot.'

"The ultimate goal of this book is for you to start associating the concept of freedom with you, and to start wondering why you and your friends don't have much of it, and for you to move out of the busy-prison into the meadows of life. There are lots of good reasons to quit school, but to my idealistic American mind, the pursuit of freedom encompasses most of them and outshines the others.

"If you look at the history of freedom, you notice that the most frightening thing about people who are not free is that they learn to take their bondage for granted, and to believe that this bondage is 'normal' and natural. They may not like it, but few question it or imagine anything different. There was a time when many black slaves took a sort of pride—or talked as if they took pride—in how well-behaved and hard-working they were. There was a time when most women believed—or talked as if they believed—that they should obey and submit to their husbands. In fact, people within an oppressed group often internalize their oppression so much that they are crueler, and more judgmental, to their peers than the oppressors themselves are. In China, men made deformed female feet into sexual fetishes, but women tied the cords to their own children's feet.

"Obviously, black and female people eventually caught sight of a greater vision for themselves, and change blazed through their minds, through laws, through public attitudes. All is not yet well, but the United States is now far kinder to people of color and mammary glands than it was a hundred years ago. What's more, these people are kinder to themselves. They dream bigger dreams, and flesh out grander lives, than picking cotton for the master or fixing a martini for the husband.

"Right now, a lot of you are helping history to repeat itself; you don't believe you should be free—in various ways, not just free of school. However, society gives you so many condescending, false, and harmful messages about yourselves that most of you wouldn't trust yourselves with freedom. It's all complicated by the fact that the people who infringe most dangerously and inescapably on your freedom are those who say they are helping you, those who are convinced you need their help: teachers, school counselors, perhaps your parents.

"Why should you have freedom?

"Why should anyone? To become human, to live fully. Insofar as you live what someone else dictates, you hardly live. Choice is a fundamental essence of life, and in the fullest life, each choice in deliberate and savored.

"Another reason you should be free is obvious. You should learn to live responsibly and joyfully in a free country."

BEINGS IN LOVE

This love of being alive comes with the territory of being human. The future history of humankind depends upon how well we learn aliveness and love of life over again from our children, and how well we let our love for them be the heart of how we organize ourselves in the world to take care of them. Let's go ahead and raise our kids to be beings, in love.

Wherever I have been with people—jails, mental hospitals, universities, corporations—I have never found a human being who didn't want to contribute to the well-being of other people. Regardless of how distorted their behavior or damaged their mind or how twisted their thinking, all human beings fundamentally want to help each other, be with each other, contribute to each other. Human beings want to celebrate being alive with other human beings who are celebrating being alive. This is fundamental to our nature as human beings. I believe that the world of human beings can eventually become conscious of, and operate according to, this fundamental love of human beings for each other and their desire to celebrate being itself-—if the mind's resistance to this doesn't destroy us first.

Our minds resist surrendering to celebration of the joy of being alive with other human beings. We have learned that human beings are dangerous. We learn this in the course of growing up. We learned it from all the warnings our parents and teachers and caretakers gave us about being careful to avoid untrustworthy people.

Most of us "over-learn" this paranoid fear of other human beings because of our parents' and teachers' poisonous moralism and misuse of their power to scare children into guarded behavior. Even after we forgive them and have no axe to grind, we can still make the assessments necessary to acknowledge that, all in all, our immediate forebears have not done that great a job of loving their children. We can tell by looking around at the world we live in. We can tell by all the damaged children who are our friends. We can tell by looking at our current—mostly dysfunctional—institutions (the legal system, schools and hospitals, for example). Most of us are depressed or anxious or angry or distracted or sick or just not happy. We were raised in a way that didn't work, and we are destined to raise our own children, for the most part, in the same way, unless we grow a little further and make a few changes.

I believe that the will of human beings toward contributing to each other is stronger than the resistive forces of their minds. I also believe that one day the force of being will be more in control of how humans live than the forces of the mind's resistance. The key to this is how well we love our children. How well we love our children is directly related to how well we have managed to forgive our parents and become capable of loving them again and of letting them love us. Most of the mistakes our parents made, and most of the mistakes of overdoing the attempt to protect us by scaring us half to death, were based on misguided love. They actually loved us but overdid the job of making sure we would be safe. They focused too much on preparing their children for any possible future catastrophe.

THE DAMAGE DONE BY PREPARING CHILDREN FOR "ADULT LIFE"

Often, preparing children for the future gets in the way of allowing them to grow. As I said before, most of the psychotherapy I have done with people has been to help them get over the damage they suffered from parents and teachers preparing them for life. Psychotherapy is largely a matter of *repairing* the damage of *preparing*. Most of my clients' educations forced them to learn their forbears' paranoia rather than allowing them to discover how to handle real situations in life. It is easy to miss out on life as it happens, while preparing for what is to come. It is also easy to learn this as a systematic model of how one ought to live. We end up like compulsive tourists, so busy taking pictures we forget to actually be there and take a look. Too much focus on getting ready for future performances of all kinds, too much focus on doing things right, too much focus on the symbolic meaning of things, often gets in the way of experience. An alternative example to that kind of education for children follows in the next chapter. It's a story Amy Silver, my former wife, wrote about our daughter Carson learning how to be responsible while pursuing something she chose to do herself, and being supported in it by a parent who loved her.

18 ❧ THE ALTERNATIVE TO PREPARING AND REPAIRING, BY AMY SILVER

"Then the child moved ten times round the seasons
Skated over ten clear frozen streams
Words like 'when you're older' must appease him
And promises of 'someday' make his dreams."

—JONI MITCHELL

"MOMMY, PRINCE CHARMING WON'T EAT!" cries Carson, bursting through the front door with a baby bottle in each hand. I look up at her. She is on the verge of tears. "Can't we give him back? I hate him!" she blurts. Carson, my nine-year-old home-schooled daughter, is raising two lambs for a sheep-farmer friend. The lambs, whose mothers lack enough milk to nurse them, are the size of big house cats, and follow Carson around the yard bleating. Carson has fed Snow White, who is now five days old, every few hours from dawn until late at night since the lamb was a few hours old, and "Snow" now greedily empties a four-ounce bottle of milk in two minutes flat. But Prince Charming, who was two weeks old when we brought him home yesterday, had given up on food after days of unsuccessful sucking on his mother's dry udder. He chews halfheartedly on the nipple, letting the milk dribble down his chin, and quits after a few seconds.

Carson has been trying valiantly every hour or so to force milk into his bony body, embracing him in her strong gymnast's arms, squatting in lamb poop and straw while shoving greedy Snow away, until an ounce has disappeared, one way or another.

"Honey, let me try," I respond, recognizing Carson's imminent breaking point. She waited for these lambs for months, calling every day to check if "her" ewes were in labor, and has sacrificed much of her life to them these past five days: rising at dawn to feed them, saying "no" to invitations to play at friends' houses, washing bottles, mixing formula, helping build their pen, and cleaning up the assorted messes that arise in their wake. I take the bottle, walk with her to the pen, and, after ten minutes of struggling with the recalcitrant lamb, manage to force another ounce of milk down his throat. "'Prince Pain-in-the-Neck' is more like it," I mutter, inspiring a giggle from my disillusioned daughter. "I think he just needs to build up his sucking muscles and get the hang of it."

"Thanks, Mom," she says, accepting the bottle I hand her, and trudges into the house to wash it.

By the next day, Prince is drinking two ounces at a feeding. Carson holds him, struggling, between her knees, jamming the nipple into his mouth, and murmuring wordless sounds of encouragement while he sucks just a few seconds longer at each feeding.

Prince Pain learned to drink from a bottle. Carson learned, once again, what she could accomplish with determination, commitment, and a little support when requested. I was reminded of home-schooling mom Mary Foley's response, when pressed for a more acceptable curriculum by the Massachusetts school authorities (who eventually sued her): "Our curriculum is 'Building Confidence, Daydreaming, and Making Mistakes.'" I read about the differences between homeschoolers and schooled kids in books, in magazines, on the Internet, in newsletters. Families and observers write that home-schooled kids are more interested in learning, more self-directed, and less peer- dependent; that school makes many kids anxious, hostile, cut off from family life, and turned off to learning. Theories about how kids learn and why the home is often a better environment for learning and growing than school changed my life, caused me to reinterpret my own education and eventually to teach my children at home.

As I watch my unschoolers learn, however, I am struck by a distinction hinted at but not spelled out in the writings of Holt, Gatto, and the other philosophers who spawned the home-schooling movement: the essential difference between home-schoolers and schooled children is that schooled kids are preparing for life, while home-schoolers are living life. Learning and the life of the mind are essential aspects of a rich and satisfying life for these kids, just as they are for well-rounded adults. But learning is not preliminary to living; it *is* living.

In our traditional view, learning is a childhood-intensive, twelve- to sixteen-year competitive training regimen designed to prepare the child for "real"—adult—life. It is the modern equivalent of an apprenticeship to a trade. All other pursuits and interests of childhood are subordinated to intellectual preparation. Each aspect of life—from art and music to health, athletics, and morality—is codified and made measurable so the state can ensure that each child receives the requisite exposure. All other activities, with the exception of religion, are considered dispensable and inessential, regardless of how they might be viewed by the child's family, let alone the child itself. Religion is generally seen as a disciplinary force and thus supportive of the state's parallel task of instilling compliance and conformity. (Paradoxically, even activities that provide the identical information and training to the school's, because outside the system, are unquantifiable and hence viewed as irrelevant.) The family and the parents are viewed as either potential allies or impediments to the purposes of the educational system and the state—either as enforcers of the school's requirements during the time when the child is physically beyond its reach, or as contemptible inepts who fail to provide the school with children who have been properly prepared for institutional life, whose behavior is insufficiently regulated by fear of home retribution, and who aren't appropriately managed in the school's attempted extension of its relentless intellectual exercises into nights and weekends.

Home-schooled children, in contrast, even most of those whose parents attempt to mimic the teach-practice-test feedback loop (which has little educational purpose other than to allow bureaucratic control of the intellectual life of millions of children), are not preparing to live, but living. Once their parents make the inevitable discovery that one or two hours a day of concentrated academic work is more than sufficient to keep pace with and surpass their schooled peers, children are just as inevitably left with the question of how to fill up the remaining hours in the day. Slowly, haltingly, the child begins to replace those concerns that occupy a schooled child: How can I get all this work done? Or how can I get out of it? Am I smart? Am I cool? How will I measure up academically, socially? How can I defend myself from hostile peers and teachers? with those that are in fact the birthright of a young human being: What am I interested in? What do I like? Of what am I capable? How competent am I now? What new thing might I discover or create?

A home-schooled child begins to discover that making music, reading, writing, painting and drawing, cooking, gardening, exploring nature, caring for animals or younger children, building things, playing word or number games, sports, dance, and social and community projects are some of the ways that human beings can fill the time not occupied by basic survival tasks. Intellectual pursuits become part of a seamless whole—a life spent doing things one loves, alone and with people whose company one enjoys, in a way that one might experience the satisfaction of contributing to the family and community while expressing and being appreciated for one's unique talents. When not usurped by institutional demands and control, a child's life develops and unfolds in relation to the child's inner rhythms and the family's values as the child masters increasingly more aspects of life and takes on increasing responsibility.

Perhaps it seems decadently modern and self-indulgent to speak of a child's right to have a satisfying life, to self-expression, and to choose her own interests. Surely before industrialization and the institutionalization of childhood, most children's lives were hard, brutal, and dominated by the demands of adults and the necessities of survival. Modern education is almost universally viewed as an enlightened advance over the social realities that preceded it, a progressive force offering social justice, gender equality, an informed populace capable of self-governance, and a caring refuge for the children of poor or abusive parents.

Indeed in industrialized, developing, or colonized nations, educational institutions may well provide such a respite to economically exploited children. Even in farming cultures, the demands of agriculture in many climates produce both the oppressive economics—allowing landowners to benefit from the labor of the disenfranchised, including children—and the brutal living conditions that can make childhood hell.

But if we look back beyond agriculture to the millennia of human hunter-gatherer culture, we may see a different picture. Anthropologists tell us that children of modern hunter-gatherer cultures are permitted a degree of freedom unknown in our society. When a child is developmentally prepared to begin to take on the responsibilities of adulthood, it learns by imitating adults. A large part of each day is spent in what we deprecate as "play —creative, skill-building activities psychologists have long recognized as the central vocation of childhood. The child is an integral part of the social, productive, and spiritual life of the village. Life skills are transmitted naturally, casually, and with a minimum of the classification and assessment so cherished by our schools. A life that is satisfying, expressive, and contributive is no more foreign to children in this quintessential human constellation than to adults, although it seems a vanity in our more "developed" society to most adults as well as to children. Our modern idea that adults should be free to find their own meaning in life, to design their own happiness, to have purposes of their own, is both very new and very old, as it is essentially about being creative, and human beings—*Homo sapiens sapiens,* our species—are defined by creativity. The people who invented art, language, culture itself in its multifarious forms did so for fifty or 100,000 years without going to school. For that matter, who's to say that language and art were invented by adults? Evidence to the contrary exists. One thing is for certain: if the children of prehistory had spent their lives in the regimented, intrusive, valuative oppression of our schools, they would have invented nothing. John Taylor Gatto, an award-winning teacher for twenty-five years who finally abandoned the system in disgust, writes:

> The logic of the school-mind is that it is better to leave school with a tool kit of superficial jargon derived from economics, sociology, natural science, and so on, than with one genuine enthusiasm. But quality in education entails learning about something in depth. Confusion is thrust upon kids by too many strange adults, each working alone with only the thinnest relationship with each other, pretending, for the most part, to an expertise they do not posses.

In contrast, I observe how Carson fills her days with an endless panoply of projects and enthusiasms, in the process accumulating more information and genuine understanding about a wide variety of subjects than many college-educated adults have. From her three-year ongoing project to paint the walls of her room with a giant undersea mural, to the numerous cages in her room filled with her reptilian and amphibious charges; from her early, awkward experiments in computer programming to her multiple writing projects including poetry, stories, letters to pen pals, and the newsletter she writes for the "Kids Clean-Up Club" she and her friends organized; her interests, like mine, are limited only by the hours in a day. She decided three years ago that she wants to be a marine biologist, and for three years she's been teaching herself about marine life, even choosing to learn Latin once she learned it would be helpful for a scientist to know. With a little guidance and support from me, her purposes are essentially her own.

John Taylor Gatto writes, " . . . discovering meaning for yourself, and discovering a satisfying purpose for yourself, is a big part of what education is. How this can be done by locking children away from the world is beyond me." I think of the famously successful people, like Einstein, about whom anecdotes are widely repeated pointing out how the person's genius went totally unrecognized in school, or like Edward Teller, who was considered a dunce and a discipline problem (and still may be, to some). These stories are usually told to illustrate the fallibility of school authorities and to encourage children (or adults) who have been perhaps unfairly categorized; the moral is that you can land in the wrong category and surprise everyone, so don't give up trying. I reach a different conclusion, however: to me, the stories illustrate that famous and successful people are distinguished partly because they have their own purposes, and they had these purposes even as children. A brilliant child with purposes of his own may, like Richard Feynman, fit easily into a school environment and be successful and admired; or a "purposeful" child may be too preoccupied with his or her own interests to bother trying to win at the school game. Either way, it is the school's complete failure to recognize any other purposes than its own that prevents it from recognizing the child's genius, not some trivial oversight on the part of a stupid teacher or two. And perhaps having a purpose is the lion's share of genius anyway.

A home-schooling family is compelled to ask, often and urgently, "What are we educating our children for? What is education's purpose? What do we see as a successful life?" As I watched Carson grapple with the ramifications of her promise to care for the two helpless, insatiable lambs, I could see her developing ability to conceive a project that excites her and then to fulfill it, to carry her vision through the inevitable obstacles, mistakes, and disappointments. This is what we are educating her for: to be an adult who, like adults for millennia, has the uniquely human capacity to invent, to create, to imagine something that does not now exist and bring it to be. This ability, for whatever reason, has somehow escaped our educational process. Creation cannot be coerced, assessed, or evaluated. It often fails, is frequently useless, and as likely leads nowhere as to a future job.

Many of Carson's innumerable projects can be translated into "academic subjects" if I need to (if forced to by the government, that is); are they therefore more valuable than her passion for making Christmas ornaments out of thistles, producing claymation films, babysitting and gardening? If I want to view her experiences through the lens of preparation—to see everything she does as having value only in terms of what it can allow her to do later—I can see most of these pursuits as useful, and some not. But if I see her life as complete and self-contained, each of her pursuits (like mine) is independently valid and valuable for its own sake.

Seeing all childhood activity as a preparation for some future, meaningful task, not as meaningful in itself, is the reverse of the related mistake we make with our own lives: seeing every adult activity as some kind of self-contained, predestined, ultimate test of who we are, instead of as one more learning process on the path of creating a life. It's as if someone declared: "Childhood is for learning, then you're graded, and you keep the same grade for life and never get to learn again." Robert Fritz, in his book entitled *Creating* (Fawcett Books, 1993), brilliantly expresses the problem:

"There are two kinds of people . . . those who see life as a performance and those who see life as a work in progress. Performers and learners. The strange irony is that our educational system is designed to produce performers, not learners. The emphasis is on successful performance rather than on successful learning. There are penalties for failure and rewards for accomplishment, as if failure and learning were separate."

This toxic association between learning and performance is what prevents so many adults from ever learning again once they escape the ordeal of compulsory schooling and forget almost everything they were ever taught. Adult—whether college graduates or high school dropouts—who would never pick up a non-fiction book or read anything on a level more complex than *Time Magazine;* who can't explain the simplest principles of science and can't remember how to do arithmetic operations, let alone algebra, statistics, or percentages; who will believe anything — the Holocaust never happened, the earth is 80,000 years old, angels and old souls and aliens can solve our problems—because they don't know how to think; who know no language but English and no music but pop, and who wouldn't dream of learning now (or learning to play an instrument, paint, recite a poem or write anything more sophisticated than a memo): these are the worried parents who try to manipulate and pressure and increasingly, drug their kids into greater compliance with the know-it-all authorities who hold the carrot of supposed future social and economic success on the stick of grades.

The same parents who once knew how boring and pointless school is now demand that their children tough it out lest they fall off the wagon of upward mobility. Having no interest in the life of the mind left themselves, they can't imagine that a child would have any natural interest in it without being forced. Their purposes are reduced to those handed them by others—to conform, to survive, and to consume.

I've learned to see my life, and my children's lives, as works in progress. No one has the right to judge our "work" but ourselves. No one can know what we need to learn but us. Our real education is in being creators, people who can bring something into being because it is worthwhile, who can form an intention and hold it, who are willing to make mistakes. Most people have not only failed to learn that by the time they emerge from their 12 to 16 years of training, they have become almost incapable of learning it from the coterie of trainers, consultants, and therapists who make their livings teaching adults what children know how to do instinctively. Learning to create may be like learning language: if it doesn't happen at the appropriate time,

Show White and Prince Charming have been returned to Fort Stover Farm to live on grass and grain. Carson (like home-schoolers all over the country whose schedules freed them to help desperate sheep farmers that spring) learned some valuable skills, lessons, and information through her lamb-nursing experience, but those aren't what made the experience worthwhile. Nursing lambs was worthwhile because that's what Carson chose to do with her time, and did. It would not be an exaggeration to say that her freedom and creativity are sacred, and that exercising them is a pure expression of the human spirit.

(Amy Silver and Grace Lewellyn have a new book, *Guerilla Learning: How to Give Your Child a Real Education With or Without School.* [John Wiley & Sons, 2001]. Read it.)

19 ‽ WHO WE ARE IS NOT HOW WELL WE PERFORM

THAT STORY ABOUT CARSON AND her lambs, and the brilliant way Amy told it, and the sensitivity and support of Carson's choices she described make me proud and happy. It also reminds me how we all seem to believe automatically in preparing for the future as more important than living in the present. This is one of the central problems of living in today's world and having a mind. In fact, I would say that believing that who we actually are is our performance, and that the primary purpose of life is to prove to others that we are good performers, are the two most dangerous values taught in schools and by parents. They are dangerous because they lead us inevitably to depression and resignation.

Therapists and consultants and teachers who know what their real jobs are, know that to get most individuals to "lose their minds and come to their senses" is the first step to curing depression. The way to overcome the doldrums taught by bad parenting and schools is to create something of your own, then to learn to love creating, then to have your work be creating like it was before schools taught it out of you. Schools cause us to end up like the computer programmer who died in the shower. He read the label on the shampoo: "Wet hair. Lather. Rinse. Repeat," and proceeded to shampoo himself to death. Like the computer programmer caught in an endless do-loop on the shampoo bottle, we are unable to escape the do-loop of the instructions we got in school. Along with the instructions came the manner of instruction, which presumed that who we are is our performance.

The pathetic truth is that teaching children what they need to learn for the future often becomes a program for living in the future, and people end up living their whole lives as a rehearsal for a time that never comes. We teach our children to spend their lives preparing to live instead of living.

OVERDOING IT

One of the big mistakes of parenting and schooling is overdoing the caretaking. In this letter I wrote to Joan, a friend of ours, after she had visited our house with her family, I speak to her about overdoing the job. Her daughter, Alita, was about five years old when I wrote this. After we talked about the letter I asked her if it would be okay if I put it in this book and she gave me permission to do so. All the names are changed, of course, but you may recognize yourself or your neighbor.

Dear Joan,

I'm writing you this letter about you and Alita because I have been thinking about the power struggles you have with her, in the context of my writing about parenting. I hope this is useful and you are not hurt or pissed off about whatever I say. If you are, please tell me so we can work through it because I really value your friendship, and since I don't always communicate exactly what I want to when I am writing, we probably need to talk to clarify and correct what I say here.

I have been thinking about you all in the back of my mind while I've been working on this book. It is useful to me because I can write better when I am thinking about real people and events. I keep thinking about that incident with you and Alita when I had invited her to go out and unload the wood from the Subaru with me. I said, "Come outside with me. I could use some help." She said, "Okay" and was going about the business of getting dressed. I had suggested she go outside with me to interrupt the struggle between you and her about her getting dressed, which it was clear you anticipated as a struggle in advance. It seems to me "getting Alita dressed" is a struggle in your mind, and turns out to be an expectation you are seldom wrong about, because you cause it to happen. You had been distracted by some conversation with Amy, and I thought I would just slip right in there and Alita and I would handle the problem by spiriting her away from the struggle.

She liked me and I asked her to come outside and help me. That was all that was necessary to get her to get dressed without a struggle. But we couldn't find her shoes. We looked around but we couldn't find them. So I said to you, "Where are her shoes?" and you responded by getting involved in the "getting dressed project" again, at which time you told her three more things she had to do to get dressed. That pretty much cranked up the struggle all over again.

You definitely work too hard at it. You take care of her more than she wants. She would learn a hell of a lot more if you could stop teaching her. You could have just answered my question or just given me the shoes. You probably interpreted my question as you would if Martin (Joan's husband) asked the question. That is, had it come from him, it really wouldn't have been just that question—it would be him asking you to take over because he was "trying hard but helpless," a sneaky strategy which I've sometimes used myself, but not as often as he does.

It appears to me that you are fearfully moralizing to Alita all the time. Your voice has a hesitancy in it and a gearing up to handle resistance before she even resists. In your voice you are sweet and condescending and fearful she'll have a fit—almost as if you are begging her not to cause trouble. You seem doubtful of your own authority. I think you are aware of this already but don't know what to do about it. I, of course, think the first thing you "should" do is stop the "shoulds." I think you are "over parenting." I think if you would give her your presence without your advice she would be less angry. If I were her I would want more than anything that you leave me alone for a minute now and then and not be telling me what I have to do next and explaining why I have to do it. Let up. In the incident where she was getting dressed to go outside you told her (I can't remember exactly) I believe, these three things, with a voice that constantly both doubted and controlled her. Which shirt to wear, which leggings to put on, which socks and shoes, along with an explanation of why she needed them. Meanwhile—while you were trying to teach her what was needed, to be sure she didn't get cold—her only concern was to escape domination by you.

Let her get cold. The cold teaches children just fine. She needs to learn from her experience, in fact she is begging to learn from her experience, and if she could get you to stop telling her what she has to do, she would be able to.

So I'm sending you this introductory chapter I've been working on because I think your over-mothering is a psychological problem of yours that many other mothers have. I think you are overdoing it out of guilt, trying to compensate for something. I don't know what you are compensating for but I'll make some guesses, most of which will be off the mark. It could be guilt for leaving your kids alone with strange caretakers too long when you went on vacations. Or you could be walking the fine line of keeping Martin happy because he is jealous of the kids' having your attention all the time (and after all, you "should be" grateful for him re-familying-up this late in his life, and you compensate him for this favor with some romance now and then). Or you could be keeping the children protected from disappointment, hurt, and the elements, trying to do better than you were done to—raise your children with less suffering than you had, being so careful to let them know you love them because you doubted whether you were loved when you were little. (Although you knew you were loved, you just couldn't understand all the hate dished out at the same time.) Or maybe you were compensating for Martin being to busy or too preoccupied or insensitive to the children.

Whatever it is, something makes you too busy doing too good a job in order to make up for not being good enough. Relax. You're already doing a hell of a lot better than you were done to. You have advanced Jewish mothering significantly beyond the Baltimore baseline. Clark (Alita's brother) and Alita will both learn, at some time in their lives, from their experience in the world, when you are not around. You could let them have the chance to learn from their experience while you are around, and only help when asked, or when there is a clear need for help that comes from them, not from your psyche.

I think this letting up on your part is critical to Alita right now to keep her from becoming an axe-murderer. Let her lead, let her work out her own way, let her not get dressed all day, let her go out in the cold without enough clothes on, do without meals, stay dirty, bug Clark and so on. Just because your standards are different from the standards you resented being imposed on you, you don't see that you are constantly harassing Alita with your own standards and expectations, in the same way you were harassed by your mother. You say she is a wild child. Fine. Build her a corral and see how she turns out. I am not talking about leaving her alone by giving her "time away" from you. I'm talking about leaving her alone when you are with her.

I know that familying is a contextual problem, and when I focus just on you and Alita I am leaving out most of the story. I know that Clark's relationship to Alita, and Alita's relationship to Martin, and Clark's to Martin and Clark's to you and yours to Martin, and the whole that is more than the sum of the parts is mostly being ignored here. I'm writing you because you are struggling the hardest and I think you need to let up the most. Gimme a call when you get this.

Love,
Brad

THE ANTIDOTE TO DOTING

An important question to ask ourselves as parents, particularly if we're doting mothers, is, "Is there any way I could find something else to do and not dote so damned much?" Quit fixing everything. Quit coaching. Quit bossing. Quit helping. Quit encouraging. What your kid understands is pretty much like that cartoon about the dog owner trying to train his dog. It shows the owner explaining in detail to Rover, in a strong voice, about what Rover did and why he is a bad dog. Then it shows, in a little balloon over Rover's head, what Rover is hearing. It's "Blah! blah! blah! Rover! Blah! blah! blah! Rover!" Modern parenting seems to involve a lot of that. We run away and leave the child with someone else, and then come back and get them and it's "Blah! blah! blah! Rover!" all over again. Get a life. Be with your kid and don't be trying to control her all the time. She has no choice but to suffocate or fight back. You are sourcing the behavior you are trying to control.

An operational definition of love is that it is simply a presence to the being of another being—much like babies teach us to love before we start training them out of it.

Marilyn Ferguson's work-in-progress called *Radical Common Sense* is about visionaries. One of the main characteristics of truly

196

visionary people is that they are good at taking care of themselves. Well, how in the hell to you learn that? How do you learn to be good at taking care of yourself? You learn it by having an opportunity to do it. Like the New York cop said, when asked, "How do I get to Carnegie Hall?"

"Practice, practice, practice!"

We learn to take care of ourselves by parents who watch over us and don't interfere except when needed, while we learn by playing around. As children grow toward getting that driver's license at sixteen, if they have been constantly and increasingly given more and more authority over their own lives, they will be ready to have full authority by then.

The basis for membership in the community of humans as a contributor rather than a drain of energy and resources is just that: practice. Children need practice in taking care of themselves. Let them have it. Support them in discovery of how to take care of themselves without doing it for them. Often friends who see you with your children can notice things about your way of being with your kids that you can't. Listen to them and ask them for advice and give your own to them freely. Raising children among a group of people who will confront you and question you about your intentions is the best way to interrupt the patterns of bad child-rearing you learned as a child. They can notice what you don't about the way you are with your children. We need each others' honest attention to do a good job of parenting. We need friends who will tell us when we are on automatic. We need to create villages (check out www.parentsoup.com). We need each other to interrupt each others' resistance to letting children grow up.

20 ✐ WHAT NOT TO DO: TRYING TO TEACH TOO MUCH TOO SOON

MORALLY PREOCCUPIED PEOPLE and institutions are sick and shallow and do severe damage to integrity at an early and vulnerable time. Often with morally strict people, and in moralistic places of instruction, children are forced to act as if they understand abstract cognitive principles (like right and wrong, good and evil, the existence of God, the concept of fairness, etc.) before they are capable of abstract cognitive thinking.

As we learned from Piaget, children do not learn the ability to generalize and abstract until about ten or eleven years of age. They learn quickly at an earlier age, however, to avoid punishment for not understanding by acting as if they understand or are trying hard to understand. Children don't know how to generalize quite like adults but they learn to be anxious about what is required of them and to feel stupid and inept. They learn this right quickly and carry it with them for a long time. They learn how to cower and play-act "sincere" effort when they are surrounded by nuns or teachers with rules and rulers, people who are twice as tall as they are. Once this phony pretense of understanding in order to avoid punishment is learned, along with being afraid all the time, it blocks any further learning. Once children finally attain the age of eleven or twelve and develop the ability to do abstract thinking, they use it to make only a few permanent defensive generalizations, one of which is "If I put on a show for the sake of the teacher, or my parents, to keep them off my back, maybe I can have another life in secret, protected by pretending to be good."

This kind of education results in a lot of moralists to torture the next generation, since none of them will be real thinkers and will have to go to a department of education or law school to get a degree and find a mate of equal ignorance from the middle and upper class. These damaged souls pair up and breed and teach school and run the court system. Their own children do okay until they leave the womb. As soon as they hit air they not only have to bear up under parenting by these folks but they are eagerly delivered to doctors, priests, parents, teachers and other patrolmen, who proceed, with all their well-intentioned ignorance, to cripple this next generation quickly before it gets beyond crippling.

Not only does moralism not work, people who are moralists and proud of it are really pathetic unhappy people, trapped in their beliefs, and a boring bunch to hang out with. One of your jobs as a responsible parent is to keep your kids away from those folks. You can't entirely, of course. But never doubt that your job as ombudsman for your child is an important one and don't let any moralist stare you down.

THE FUNDAMENTAL ASSUMPTION OF FEELING WHOLE

People who are happy in life learned, early or later in life, an assumption they roll out of bed with every day. They wake up into an assumption that something interesting, something challenging, something good, something fun is likely to happen today. Wouldn't it be great if the next generation of people, raised by us, could wake up every morning with an expectation that is vague but always there, that this day is to be looked forward to? Feeling whole is a fundamental necessity for being a creator.

Children learn first, as a natural consequence of their development, to locate themselves in the real world of sensate reality in the moment. Then, because we are usually in a hurry, we train them out of it. We do this automatically in the course of our days of living together. For example, let's say it is morning and everyone is getting ready for work and school. A child, six years old, notices something and comments; "That toothpaste smells good," when she's brushing her teeth. Parents who are attentive to their child as a constant guru of living in the moment would then themselves notice the smell of toothpaste, something they hadn't noticed for a long long time, and say, "Yep. It sure does," in a grateful and happy tone of voice. Parents in a hurry to get the kid off to school in order to get-off-to-work-to-then-get-to-the-next place-they-have-to-go-to-get-through-the-day-and-get-the-day-over-with, would say, "Hurry up, honey. We're going to be late."

The systematic teaching of hysteria about time is a part of the curriculum for the day, on most days, for most of the children in our culture. The parents of millions of children wake up into the frenetic assumption, "I have to make everybody get there on time."

They resentfully force themselves to push the kids to get ready in time, resenting children for "dawdling" while being afraid of what the boss will think if they're late again. Somehow, to be good parents, we have to interrupt that interruption. Every time a child interrupts your mental agenda to point out something they have noticed in the moment, follow their lead instead of overriding their discovery because your agenda is more important. Your agenda isn't more important. Your culture has given you a bullshit agenda. You've been torn loose from the continuum of being and captured by intellect. We are all psychotic with regard to time and money. We have to notice how we are teaching our children to be like us. We have to notice that particularly when even we don't want to be like us.

Children who are "spoiled" in the old paradigm way of thinking are actually the ones who have been raised the best. They have been taught to expect that the world is a place of nurturance and love, and as they gradually—over about twelve to sixteen years—take over full responsibility for their lives, they develop their skill in taking care of themselves in the context of an assumption of each day bringing a new and interesting adventure.

Children do a lot of fantasy play to develop their imaginations. Our job is to play along with them. Help them develop their ability to envision the future and to live into those visions themselves.

One of the things Marilyn Ferguson says in her great book, *Radical Common Sense,* is that in her extensive study of visionary people she found that "Consciously or unconsciously, they have learned to be good parents and teachers to themselves." I think this is more than likely related to them not having had their natural-born optimism stomped out of them at an early age by parents hysterical about time and money.

It doesn't hurt to let children lead every now and then. Just do whatever they do or ask you to do. You'll learn how to play with them the way they like to play at whatever age they are. Play with them. They will teach you again to be a visionary, thereby allowing you to envision how to raise them.

RADICAL PARENTING

Radical Parenting is staying connected with your child as an older being to a younger being. To be present to a child's presence to you, to notice that you are being noticed, and to give your full attention with no particular agenda, is one of the great joys of parenting. You and your child can play with your developing minds together, bonded as one noticing being noticing another. As Kierkegaard said, "A person who relates to another person and relates also to that relationship relates thereby to God." In other words, a being who relates to another being, and relates to that relationship, relates thereby to all of being. You discover yourself in relation to that little being and through that, at the same time love all of being. Children are rich with the fullness of being, and the nurturance you get from nurturing them is the best there is. This is more valuable than money. People who get mildly stoned and play with their kids for hours instead of making more money are looked down upon in this culture. To me, if they don't overdo the getting stoned part, they are damned near ideal parents.

My friends and I are taking on the central problem of raising a generation of human beings, the world over, who are prepared to love and share with other human beings. What we can all do to help the world become a much better place is to take delight in our children, and, viewing them through the eyes of delight, work consciously to have them love life and learning and other people. We do this more by example than instruction.

The good life is shared problems. Solving big problems together is the best game on earth. If parents and teachers start teaching the fun of playing with problems, help for the whole world is on the way. This is the problem we now face: New York (Reuters Health): More than one quarter of U.S. teenagers are highly dissatisfied with their lives, according to the results of a recent survey. And researchers say this unhappiness puts them at increased risk for violent and aggressive behavior.

"In the survey of more than 5,000 public high school students in South Carolina, about 30% of black males and females, 28% of white females and more than 26% of white males reported low levels of satisfaction with life overall.

"White females who were dissatisfied were nearly four times more likely than their satisfied peers to have carried a gun to school in the past month, and were twice as likely to have fought at school in the past year, the report indicates.

"Similarly, dissatisfied white males and black males and females were nearly twice as likely to have carried a weapon in the past month, the investigators found. Dissatisfied black males were more than three times more likely to have been involved in a physical fight that required medical treatment."

The survey results are published in a recent issue of the *American Journal of Health Behavior* (2001, v. 25, p. 353–366).

"There are some very unhappy kids out there, and their lack of life satisfaction shows up in violent and aggressive behaviors," lead study author Dr. Robert F. Valois, a psychologist at the University of South Carolina in Columbia, explained in a statement.

It is not clear whether dissatisfaction with life leads to violent behavior or if the reverse is true. Teens in general may have trouble managing stress, making decisions and communicating, which can cause frustration and raise the risk of behaving aggressively, the study's authors point out.

"Adolescents dissatisfied with life might engage in physical fighting as a result of poor communication skills and the inability to manage stress, resulting in poor conflict resolution and a physical altercation," Valois and colleagues write.

The survey, conducted for the US.. Centers for Disease Control and Prevention, also asked teens to rate their levels of satisfaction with their families, friends, school experiences, living environment and themselves. The satisfaction scale ranged from "delighted" to "terrible."

Adolescents tended to report the most dissatisfaction with school. They were more satisfied with their family, friends, living environment and themselves. The way to approach this problem is in the next step, envisioning a possible future.

Step VI

Getting Good at the Ongoing Vision and Re-Vision of What Could Be

21 ❧ ILLUSIONS CAN BE OUR FRIENDS IF WE KNOW THEY ARE NOT REAL

AFTER WE EVOLVED THE CAPACITY to create labels for reality and to separate our labels from reality itself, we developed the ability to make maps of our remembered experiences. That allowed us to tell stories about what happened and to imagine what might happen. We became capable of having illusions. Illusions are our friends if we can just get one point: Illusions are for creating, not for self-assurance.

Living in a story is what we all must do because we are human. Human beings live in the real world, but always in a way consistent with some story. Most of us live in stories that were created for us by our provincial culture and the conditions of life we started out in and survived in as children. Some of us grow beyond that and, as adults, *actually participate in the design of the story out of which we live.*

Most human beings all over the planet live their entire lives trapped in a story, rather than co-creating a new one. The stories most of the people you and I know were desperately contrived in order to endure the circumstances of middle- or lower- or upper-class child abuse in western culture. Those of us who have transcended our culture and how we were raised to some extent have found that living in a story of our own conscious creation is actually not bad. It's a hell of a lot less miserable than living in the survival story we came out of childhood with.

When we shed the extant delusional system of our time, it is scary. The culture we grew up in tells us our life has a particular meaning. It tells us how we must be careful to avoid symbolic dangers, how we should compete to overcome our adversaries, be polite above all else, maintain our belief in God, and so on. There are thousands of bullshit beliefs of all kinds people have been selling as reality in our culture for centuries. When we get over attachment to the illusion of who we are, which our culture has taught us, we get to create some new illusions for the future.

We don't have any choice not to live by illusions. It is our given destiny to be delusional. It's out of these illusions of a possible future that we live the creative and intentional life.

Creation of the future with conscious illusions (called visions) works best if the illusions meet two criteria:

(1) They involve making a contribution to other people in some way, and

(2) They closely match the survival skills from our individual past, because maintenance and upkeep for those illusions are already developed and the habit structure can be used.

A person who understands the use of illusion from a position of transcendence or detachment—that is, a person who uses illusions but doesn't believe in them—has a much happier and more fulfilled life. If I have to be disappointed about an image I just dreamed up in the first place, it's quite different than feeling like dying because somebody disappointed or rejected who I believe myself to be.

When a person can use illusions to design their future in a playful and creative way, they can design a life and education for their children in cooperation with the children themselves and at the same time model for the children what creating with vision consists of. The same fundamental grounding in experience in the body that children have naturally is what the parent needs in order to have enough detachment to use her mind rather than be used by her mind.

RADICAL BEING

We come into existence as beings and grow minds, which eventually come to so dominate the experience of being that there is little time or space left to attend to any aspects of life other than thought. The books I have written before this one were dedicated to attempting to undo damage already done by moralistic parenting. For the child raised by the standard cultural Nazi parent, the mind becomes a jail. Being in jail is worrisome and depressing. The primary cause of most anxiety and depression is being trapped in the mind, unable to notice because of constantly thinking. We stay trapped in our minds because of various kinds of lying—outright lying, hiding, lies of omission, pretense, little white lies, withholding, yadda yadda yadda. Lying keeps you trapped in the jail of the mind and we all lie like hell all of the time.

My clients in psychotherapy over the years have reflected the culture they grew up in. They had all been taught systematically to lie by the way they were parented and educated. The only thing that could rescue them from the jail of the mind was to start telling the truth: about everything they had done, everything they felt and everything they thought. Telling the truth gets you back out into the real world, where you can deal with other people and feelings to some degree of completion before you recreate the next mess in your life out of the unfinished business from the last completion you avoided.

Human stress is caused by the mind of the individual suffering from stress. Suffering comes from being trapped in the mind, unable to escape the categories you have made up for yourself and others, the emotional attachment to ideas you invented to protect yourself from feelings in the past, and the ranting and raving of the mind.

This fundamental dis-ease of being trapped in the mind is what I have called moralism. Moralism is extreme attachment to moral principles—being trapped in the valuational continuum where judgments about right and wrong and good and bad are given excessive significance and emotional charge. These principles become more important than life itself.

The suffering that comes from this attachment to ideals is universal, goes across class lines and is immense. *The largest economic enterprise on planet earth is illegal drugs, most of them pain-killers.* One of the largest legal enterprises on the planet is the pharmaceutical industry, a large proportion of which manufactures pain killers and anti-depressants. Various experts in addiction, quoted in *The Paradigm Conspiracy* by Breton and Largent estimate that at least *half of the population of the world is addicted to either some substance, or some compulsive process.*

What does this mean? Well, I think it means there are a lot of people who are in pain and want to do something about it. I think that most of the suffering comes from living in stories that don't fit, and trying to make reality fit the stories. I don't think education usually helps with this. I think it usually makes things worse. People who are educated come up with something like "the war on drugs" to handle this problem, because the moralism that is the source of the problem is the only thing they have to approach the problem with.

As I said, we all have the disease of moralism. Given that, the secret of the good life is learning how to manage the disease like one manages herpes or diabetes or other incurable but controllable diseases. Most of us keep repeating the same kind of behavior in relation to other people and ourselves, begging, berating, scolding ourselves and each other and our children, trying to convince everyone that if we would all just live up to our expectations we'd be happy. We do this over and over again and expect a different result each time. We get the same result: anger, discomfort, depression, anxiety, and somatic ailments due to stress. Like the programmer who died in the shower when he read the instructions on the shampoo (Wet hair. Lather. Rinse. Repeat.), we have been all been caught in a do-loop, shampooing ourselves to death. Our instructions are something like, "Make baby. Moralize. Repeat." Most parents believe that the primary responsibility of parenting is moralizing intensely and repeatedly. This is the worst piece of delusional bullshit extant today. This is the core source of middle-class child abuse.

OLD-TIMEY PARENTING

Your parents did the best they could, given that they lived in the dark ages, where male intellect reigned supreme, with no respect for the continuum of genetic learning from which we came. You've probably survived well enough to go on to have children of your own, but your method of survival still probably limits you much more than necessary. You are very likely to be more worrying and worrisome than necessary, trying to fill up emptiness with good behavior to get brownie points along the way as a pathway to happiness. You might already know that being trapped in performance mode is pretty screwed up but you're raising your kids the same way anyhow. If we can start over again from a new set of premises we have a chance of having the buck stop here.

GROWING

Human development is a continuum of growth of the mind out of the being (when we are babies), through a period in which the mind captures all our attention (adolescence) and then to a time in which the liberation of the being from domination by the mind occurs (maturity). The full path of growth from birth to maturity consists of the birth of being, the growth of the mind, a period of domination of the being by the mind, and finally, a mind used by the being who has escaped domination by the mind.

How capable we are in keeping body and soul together as adults is directly contingent upon staying in touch with the experience of being in the body—noticing, moving, playing, manifesting energy —doing things other than thinking. Happiness and freedom for both you and your child depends upon not losing touch with being in the body and in the world, as you grow your minds.

As a psychotherapist my main therapeutic method (for people who had been torn loose from contact with being and were trapped in their minds and kept out of contact with being) was coaching people to tell the truth. When people begin telling the truth about what they have done, what they feel, and what they think, they free themselves from the jail of their own mind.

It's lying that keeps one from gaining freedom from domination by one's own mind. When a person who was once divided against herself, and out of touch with the joy of living, becomes whole again through psychotherapy, it is the result of beginning to notice things in the world all over again, including her own body, and running her life more in obedience to what she notices, than in obedience to interpretations she has worked hard to brainwash herself with. She reports her mind's machinations to others, simply to share with others (including others she's thinking about), but she doesn't have much faith in her mind as a source of directions.

When one who has been damaged by how she was raised begins to heal and become whole again, the healing is a result of establishing balance out of imbalance, a reunification of being and mind. A person who has become whole again makes the best parent. The problem is, most kids are born before their parents are over their own raising enough to feel whole. Often, having the baby is an attempt to do just that. Sometimes it works. Most of the time it doesn't work. In that case, there are some things you can do to help yourself. One is to let that baby be your teacher.

EMERGENCY PSYCHOTHERAPY

When a person "loses their mind and comes to their senses" in psychotherapy there is a period of troublesome disorientation. Reorientation occurs through getting back in touch with gravity, sensation, and what Wilhelm Reich and Fritz Perls called "organismic self-regulation."

To become grounded in experience again is not just changing some opinions. Opinions do change but that is after the reorientation to experience has occurred. *You start living from what you notice you want rather than what your mind says you should want.*

Thinking itself becomes merely something else to notice and use, once one has become reoriented to experience. Thinking loses its prior status as a primary ruler and jail-keeper of being and becomes more like the chauffeur. The *mind* becomes background and the *being in the body* is in the foreground, very much like the children are in the first place. So when you're thirsty you get a drink, when you're hungry you eat, when you're tired you rest, and when you have to go to the bathroom you go. You notice other people's expressions and tone of voice and changes in coloring and pace of speech, etc. You are centered in the world of noticing as the foreground and your opinions are in the background—and changing constantly!

Human development is a continuum of growth of the mind out of the being, and then the liberation of the being from domination by the mind. How can we allow minds to grow without losing touch with being? What is the best way to raise children so that they don't have to be torn loose from their grounding in being? Young humans must go through a long period of growth of a mind, and parenting and teaching must assist them in this task, but can they do it without breaking loose from the nourishment of commonplace experience? Children can learn whatever values the culture they are dumped into has for sale, without having their spirit crushed.

Luckily, through sharing honestly, some of us have learned from each other a few things that we know don't work. We know that moralizing constantly with children at an early age makes chronic liars out of them in their adulthood. We know that enforcing rules with a vengeance damages people and makes for a miserable life. Stringent moral instruction at an early age doesn't result in a happy whole adult. Stringent moral instruction at an early age results in miserable, self-righteous, phony, manipulative, sick and stupid people.

Phony, unhappy parents and teachers, enforcing rules with a vengeance, damage children. Each damaged child has another miserable life out of which come more children, who get mistreated in the dysfunctional ways of the tradition. Many among us know that stringent moral instruction at an early age doesn't work but it's mostly the dumbest of our lot who become teachers in charge of the children. Most of them don't have a clue about the damage they do with their "shoulds" and their conditional love and their insipid moralism.

Even parents who know better continue to damage their children in spite of what they know. We find ourselves, in trying to help our children, acting on automatic based on how we were raised. Often, out of love for them, mixed with anger, expressed through stringently enforced cautionary rules, taught at too early an age for the child to comprehend, we teach them the same anxieties that were trained into us.

This raises a whole bunch of question. These questions allow us to *use our minds* to design a new kind of life for ourserves and particularly our children. Once we ourselves have changed our identity from our "performance" to our *being,* we can use our minds to design a new future. we can focus on how we might design a better way for children to be raised so they don't have to suffer so much. What if children were allowed to discover how to take care of themselves?

What if parents had faith enough in themselves and their children to simply protect children while they unfold as they were genetically programmed to do, instead of forcing them, with punishment and shame, to be worried and afraid, and to memorize rules "for their own good"? What would happen if love and encouragement and an even-handed permission to experiment are given to children, based on assuming they are okay to start with, rather than assuming they are evil little hog-faced pleasure-seekers who need to be taught how to behave?

What if parents were in a therapeutic community in which their tendency to take out their misery on their children in the name of love was compassionately interrupted? What if the world became such a therapeutic community?

Changes in the way we all live together can happen through a radical change in how we raise our young. If love and encourage-ment works, and I say it does, maybe it could become the norm, and we could reorganize the whole human community and create the pos-sibility of a lifetime of play and service for every human being on the planet.

This has radical implications for any individual who right now wants to save his own life and the life of his child from well-inten-tioned but misery-making caretakers. If you have to, quit work. Move to the country or a small town. Take your kids out of school and raise them yourself. Home-school them and trade care-taking with other home-schooling families or single parents. Make friends with some strangers who are doing the same thing you are doing to escape the poisoning of their culture. Make some kind of living by doing some-thing that gives you back your connection with the earth and with all the people you got torn loose from by your education. Allow your children to stay in touch with gravity and their bodies and you and each other. Be there for them to snuggle with. Do this at any cost.

Be a radical. Get back to the juice at the root of things. Learn from your children and don't try to teach them a damned thing unless they ask. You yourself were trained out of some of the best things you will ever know. Learn some of those things over again from your child. Once upon a time when you were very young you had integrity. You were trained out of that and given the disease of moralism as a substitute. Escape while you still can, and take your children with you.

22 ❧ THE VISION OF A NEW KIND OF CHILDHOOD FOR HUMAN BEINGS

YOU READ A LITTLE BIT about my psychological history in the beginning of this book. But who I am is not that psychological history anymore. I have discovered who I am, and who you are, and it transcends our stories. Who I am is this: I am a being who notices. Considering my identity to be the being who notices, and who has a particular psychological history, allows me to choose how I use that history. That history can be used for creating a life for the being I am and for the beings I am in community with.

I can choose how I live, rather than just react to my past for the rest of my life. I have chosen, instead of just reacting to my past, to live from a vision I have created with some friends, which is in the future rather than in the past. Here is the vision from which we now live:

We envision a world where all the children in the world are supported by adults who are noticers. These noticers are paying attention to what the child is looking for next, out of curiosity, and then finding ways to support the child on that curiosity and learning track. It may be as simple as handing her a Lego or as complicated as getting her hooked up with the sources she needs on the Internet. The whole world we envision is organized around that particular kind of activity—noticing and providing what is needed.

Adults who have learned from raising kids this way and kids who are being raised this way, live in communities of families. All the people in the community get treated the same way the children are treated: with honor to the being who is a learning and living being. All the people are doing whatever they can to support each other in the continuous endeavor called learning and creating. All of the economic, political, educational, governmental and social structures are organized to support this model of how people treat their children and how they live together.

Every child born on earth is born into the possibility of a lifetime of play and service. The restoration of ecological balance, the end of starvation on the planet, the end to war and the military industrial-centered economy, the end of racial prejudice, of top down management, of schools and a justice system that fills prisons—all this will come about as a natural result of this reordering of priorities based on the quality of attention and contact between parents and children, and the honoring of each other as beings by adults.

That is our vision. And we're sticking to it. If you learn to parent from reading this book, you are in danger of becoming a member of a cult which plans to take over the world. We are for the end of brainwashing children according to whatever set of beliefs they happen to be dumped into when born. We want to have substituted, for that provincialism, the rearing of children with real love, from the beginning, through careful attention to the cues provided by the children themselves and our natural response to them as they unfold.

HOW WE WERE ABLE TO COME UP WITH A VISION

My friends and I are able to envision such a world as being possible out of our own personal transformation. From people trapped in the jail of our own reactive minds, we became beings who possess their own minds. Our minds have come to be employed by paying attention. We grew up. We found that growing up has to recur on a daily basis and that there is no end to growing until death. We have been telling each other the truth about our experience of being here. We have been radically honest about what we have done, what we think and what we feel. We have learned to pay attention first to who and what is present and what we want and what those around us want. We have learned to search out the means to support others and ourselves in pursuing the paths that peak our interest and that get us what we want. We are already living this way. We are a community of friends who support each other in radical honesty and the intimacy that comes from being honest. To keep living this way we are committed to interrupting each other's minds whenever we get lost in mistaking categories of experience for experience itself. We are raising our children with less stress on the importance of beliefs. We, who were taught that having the right beliefs was the most important thing in the world, no longer believe that. We think paying attention is more important than belief. We are committed to each other and to a common vision of a world, where living this way is possible for every human creature on earth.

At the heart of this vision and the community formed around it is a picture. It is a simple picture of children and adults playing together. We see children whose path of learning is directed by their curiosity, with support from their parents and caretakers who work to provide for them what they need next, each step of the way to adulthood. The society and community within which these parents and children live is organized around the principle of paying attention to children and to the fundamental child-like being of adults.

We are bringing this vision into being in how we live and work together, and we are committed to having this transformation for the whole world, before we die.

There is a lot of work to do, but then again there are a lot of people to do the work. You can help and we want you to. If we can help you happily raise your kids while honoring the little beings they are, you will be helping us bring about our vision of a world where people are all organized in such a way, and committed to treating each other kindly and with love. We think the best way to change the world is by raising our kids this way. The new world we envision starts right now, and treating other adults the same way starts right now as well. Honoring the being of human beings, we think, is the key to a good life and a new kind of world.

LET US KNOW YOU ARE THERE AND KEEP IN TOUCH

Let us know what and how you are doing with your children. Let's figure out how to support each other. That is all it takes for the transformation of the world to occur. The details of changing the social, political and economic structures will be worked out in the context of our mutual commitment to this vision.

This way of treating children and each other is quite different than the conventional stress on mere intellectual learning. The intellect develops fine, and with more joy than usual, when it is not pushed so hard by parents and teachers as a critical method of self-protection and survival. Nurturing children's spirits is more important for their freedom than anything we can teach them intellectually.

The being of the parent loves the being of the child, consciously, and then two free persons grow and grow and grow. The first generation ever of independent people, not enslaved by their own minds, is born. Beings are in charge of their own minds, rather than minds in charge of their own beings.

This is the dawning of the age of enlightenment. We and our

children can bring a new way of living for human beings. Many of us think that if we don't, humanity itself will come to an end. Let's enjoy this dawning of enlightenment through love, and save ourselves and our loved ones and the world we all live in from the death-dealing tradition we were all born into, from our minds, from our moralism, from ourselves.

STEP VII

THE INTEGRATION AND APPLICATION
OF WHAT WE HAVE LEARNED
FROM OUTGROWING OUR CULTURE

23 ❧ THE FIRST TRUTH, THE TRUTH OF THE EXPERIENCE OF BEING

"The world is my womb, and my mother's womb was my first world."

—R. D. LAING

WE GRADUALLY BEGIN TO THINK of ourselves, in the course of growing up, as personalities made up of all the lessons we have learned. Our hard-earned lessons count heavily in our consideration of who we are. Unless we mature to a further stage of growth than adolescence, we complicate our lives by holding on to these hard-earned lessons long after they have outlived their usefulness. Take, for example, the child who learns to persistently beg his mother in a whiny voice, first for cookies, and later for the keys to the car. Since it worked with Mom, and since Dad left most of that up to Mom, he keeps using what works. At age forty, he may still be treating his third wife the same way without having acheived those same results for years.

The mind doesn't like to change itself in the face of new information. Lessons learned and held on to in this fashion make up the personality to which we are shackled. This makes life harder than it has to be. The way out of this suffering is to expand who we consider ourselves to be. We must return to being more than the personalities we have shrunk to during the course of growing up.

By the time we are old enough to ride a bike we are personalities. In the course of learning to be personalities we forget something we knew before we had any vested interest in behaving consistently: the sense of unity in the womb, before we knew we existed as independent beings.

This is how we all began: the earth happened and chemistry brought us to be. After a long period of evolution, you and I showed up. After about the first four or five months in the womb, we had our first experience of being: a dawning of consciousness.

The first experience we all had was when life came on. Dawn seems to be the best metaphor for this. Dawn happens in a slow and almost indistinguishable way, a long time before sunrise. The light of life came on for us, in the same way, a long time before birth. The Hindus call consciousness the light that enlightens the light, or the light that allows us to see light. The womb is where this light, our consciousness, first occurred. For the first time we experienced experience itself. The gradual accumulation of light made it impossible to say when day happened, but suddenly it was there. That is, we were our experience. The fetus matured until the wiring was complete and suddenly experiencing *was*. What we were in the womb was a unity of experiencing.

This unity of experience went on for an eternity. In our time, the time we know about now, it was four or five months. Then it was an eternity. It was eternity because it was everything we knew. We never forget that time, but we have no way of remembering it in a way we can describe. It is indefinable, unrememberable in any graspable way. It is a record of unitary experience without limits. All religions, gods, metaphysics, theologies, philosophies, and teachings of masters of all faiths could be attempts to remember these eternal months past, this lost sense of unity.

Since the beginning of human history, priests have been trying to put this sense of unity into words, trying to communicate about the ineffable, trying to articulate a limbic experience. They knew something was there, but didn't know how to talk about it, yet couldn't resist trying. And the more they talked, the more confusion arose between the attempt to define unity and the actual experience of unity. As a result of our inability to put it into words, this experience of oneness, a commonplace experience, has become highly overrated. It has come to be called enlightenment.

Enlightenment is knowing unity. Enlightenment is not being able to talk about unity. The philosophy of enlightenment is talking about or trying to describe the experience of unity.

Unity is the nature of things. It doesn't take any work. It is a given. We are each creators of the universe out of our own being. What is given us to experience is a unity, within which we make distinctions. The sound we hear when our ears are stopped up is the electrical generator of unity. When our eyes are closed, the darkness we see is the generator of unity. When our eyes are open whatever we see is who we actually are. As Krishnamurti says, "you are the world." From the moment life starts, the being we are constantly creates the world with its senses. The world grows and the mind grows out of this unity. The world is created for us out of our fundamental equipment—our being.

We are constantly creating the world by merely perceiving. When we hear, we are creating sound. When we see, we are creating what is seen in our visual cortex. When we integrate sight, sound, smell, touch, balance, and movement, our involuntary nervous system creates the world. When we die, for all practical purposes, the world ends. We are each, without any effort whatsoever, creators of the world. But since we do it effortlessly, and everybody does it, it doesn't count for much in our considerations of who we are. Usually we consider creating meaning to be more important than creating the world. We take for granted our function as creators of the world and focus much more attention on creating meaning. We are preoccupied with the power of interpretation. We are much more interested in our uniqueness, derived from what we have worked to learn, than in the source of our power as creators.

It is our fate as human beings to grasp after the ineffable, trying to regain a lost sense of unity. Even so, when we do get in touch with unity, the vastness of our being, for a few seconds, we usually run like hell. We feel as if we are about to lose something. We are. We are about to lose the protection and safety of the limited definition of self we have come to think we are. We are afraid of losing who we think we are, which is special, and we are afraid of becoming who we actually are, which is not special, even though godlike in power.

When we become aware of ourselves as indefinable, uncategorizeable, simple creators of the world, we lose all certainty. Being present to the immediate moment-to-moment passing of the world, the fragility of our own being, and the relative unimportance of the personality we think we are, is a terrifying experience. Being fully aware of our ever-present, ever-changing existence throws us into the same ineffable state as when the light came on while we were unseeing in the womb. Simultaneous awareness of the life of being, and the lesser importance of the personality to which we have become attached, is a second enlightenment that comes to all humans who grow up beyond the stage of adolescence. But it feels like dying. To avoid the trauma of it, the great majority of us remain adolescents until the end of our lives.

This is not a minor philosophical point. This is the heart of the matter. Most of us would rather kill ourselves than be, particularly if who we think we are keeps dying. Many of us do.

THE BIRTH OF BEING

Go back for a moment in your imagination and memory to the beginning. There are sounds like intestines rumbling. Sensations of various kinds are starting. There is a vague sense of movement. There are voice sounds, like dolphins calling to each other under the sea. In this beginning, there is no seeing, thus no dark. To the unborn there is no knowledge of darkness because there is no light and no mind to contrast dark and light. Experiences in this unseeing world are the basis upon which we begin to form the mind.

Here, in a "background" which is all that we are, which lasts however long we do, we are our beginning. You can go back here anytime you like. I often do when I meditate.

Much later, a true eternity later, the experiences of birth, light, air, breathing and pain flood the being. The mind begins to be born out of this ocean of experience—even before birth. After seven months in the womb, the unborn baby is capable of learning to respond in a predictable fashion to outside stimuli, such as sound. Laboratory experiments have found that a seven-month-old fetus will react to an electrical shock to the mother's womb with a full contraction. When this shock is applied along with a loud sound, the fetus is conditioned, after only a few trials, to go into a full contraction at the loud sound, without any electrical shock. An association between the sound and shock is made; therefore learning has occurred. So now we know (thanks to evil scientists who have tortured fetuses in this manner) that the mind begins to form, from associations between ebbs and flows in the ocean of experience, prior to birth. This grouping of replicated experiences begins to form the mind.

Sometime shortly after birth we demarcate a little area, a smaller sea, from our ocean of experience. We distinguish our mother's breast, our mother, our hand, our body, our clothes, our bed. We become a sea of suggestions. We grow up all the rest of the way surrounded and protected by this expanding sea of suggestions, and eventually, thousands of refinements later, a group of suggestions becomes who we think we are.

Who we actually are, of course, remains always more than the mental images we form while growing up. First we are the experiencer of what is momentarily present; second we are the multi-sensory recorder of experience; last, and less importantly, we are the rememberer. Later, we are most focused on remembering our own reputations. But who we always really are, from the beginning, is a context, a parenthesis, a being who creates the world for itself by sensing. We are the being self, the source of being and remembering. Re-contacting that basic beginning sensate self rescues us from the mind—the murderer, and potential ally, within.

GETTING BORN AGAIN

As you may recall, we have all had a lot to deal with in order to grow up to adulthood. After forming a personality and losing touch with the wholeness of being, we then rediscover wholeness, but experience it as a threat to our personality. Personality can eventually be included in the wholeness of being, but not without some hard work that requires courage and takes a while. It is a process of disintegration and reintegration. Some people call it dying and getting born again.

The creator being is the being that came alive in the womb at four or five months after conception, when the wiring was complete and the light came on. We forget this being rather quickly. In just a few years we are so surrounded by our creation, the sea of suggestions, we can hardly touch or taste or smell or feel or see the ocean of experience that still surrounds us. We forget we live in a sea that is a part of an ocean. We forget we are the source of the whole ocean. Getting born again is remembering that.

There is a yearning implicit in being born human. It becomes clear in summarizing what we've said so far: We awaken in the womb into an ocean of experience. Over a long period of rime, that ocean of experience becomes a sea of suggestions. We lose track of the ocean of experience. We lose track of having created the sea. After we have lost track of everything sufficiently, we continue to interact with the sea and create a self. What we call the "self" is a creation of further interactions of the sea of suggestions. The being we were when we began, the being we actually still are, alive in an ocean of experience, including all the ocean as itself, recedes to the background of our attention, and the "self" we have created comes to the foreground. As we identify with our newly created self, we lose touch with the being we are and have been since the light came on. It could be that all religious, poetic, romantic or transcendental experiences can be accounted for by a kind of yearning to recapture completely the four-to-nine month time-lapse photograph of being we developed in that eternal time in the womb. A kind of fused multi-sensory recording, made before our senses themselves were distinct, resides in each of our memories; a remembrance of unity.

This undistinguished unity lasts some time past birth until the baby breaks the world into two pieces with its first concept based on replicated events. That first concept may come after being fed at mother's breast many times. At some point the memory of previous events of warmth, milk, cuddling, sucking, and swallowing becomes distinguished from all other memories, and the baby cries to be fed. At that point, if the baby gets fed and remembers it, the next time the baby is hungry and cries again, he or she enters time—and a life of increasing distinctions. The global world of experience becomes divided into "feeding events" and "nonfeeding events." The unity we all search for, the peace that passeth understanding and the looked-forward-to heaven and reunion with God, is a vague but all-pervasive memory of a time of bliss, yearningly remembered from the past, and longingly projected forward to the future.

This yearning for something that can't quite be remembered in the way we usually remember is constantly triggered by the ever-present and ever-current background experience of being. When we close our eyes and cover our ears, we can hear our own heartbeat and hum. It stimulates remembrances of times past that can't be conceptualized. From thee we come. To thee we go.

There is a Zen story about two fishes arguing about the existence of the ocean. The first fish says, "It's all around you. You are surrounded by water. You have lived in water all of your life."

"Show me! Prove it! Where is this ocean?" the second fish demands. The difficulty in being aware of the perpetual, continuous, taken-for-granted, sustenance of being is that it has been there since the light first came on. We have nothing with which to compare it. There is no measure of its existence.

The ever-present ocean of experience has no inside or outside. Inside us and outside us are both inside us. Who we are is the being within which occurs that experience we call "inside our body" and that experience we call "outside our body." More accurately, we are the inside and outside experience itself, happening. We learn to distinguish "inside" and "outside" an eternity after the light first comes on (because then we had no concept of time) and years after we are born. (It takes an eternity plus a couple of years before our minds distinguish "inside" and "outside.")

The mind is the sea of suggestions we learned as we grew. The mind is born out of the indefinable ocean of experience we first were and still are. The sea of suggestions we come to think we are as personalities is itself in a larger ocean, like the original ocean of experience, currently obscured by the sea of suggestions we consider ourselves to be.

To be whole, we must recontact the being we are and were and evermore shall be until the end of each of our times. That being is the creator being—the background hum that keeps us cooking, the basic circuit board, the baseline buzz, the limbic connection. The cognitive faculties of the mind are a secondary development for steering, not the primary driving force of life. As we develop minds they lead us away from the experience of being, and religious practices were developed to get us back to it. Religions were developed to help us get back home to the hum we started with.

Meditation, sitting quietly until the mind settles down, brings a sense of wholeness. I believe the primary value of meditation is that while meditating we reunify the memory of our first sense of being with our current breathing, heart-beating, sensate, present tense experience of being. Being a living being, "knowing" in our bones that we have been being for some time, is the heart of who each of us is. We are beings alive behind the mask of personality. Sitting in the Zendo (a place of meditation), that is what we find when we let ourselves be.

Marilyn Ferguson says, "Those who want direct knowledge, the mystics, have always been treated more or less as heretics . . . Now the heretics are gaining ground, doctrine is losing its authority, and knowledge is superseding belief." Mystics are people who rediscover experience. Belief is the sea of suggestions about who we think we are. The path from doctrine to knowledge is a development beyond doctrine. Psychotherapy was invented to try to keep body and soul together— to help us to not mind being all the time and to not be minding all the time. Good parenting does the same thing.

In the course of growing to adult size, we all have to learn the roles and rules. In order to do this, we forget, subsume, take for granted, ignore, or drop consciousness of our essential being. The path to the good life leads on further than adolescent moralism, but a lot of people don't go that far. The path from doctrine to heresy is a natural growth—a natural evolution—a transition from one level of maturity to another. Very few of us stay on the path, however, because we get so damaged by those who teach us the doctrine. We become so filled with hate, and so embroiled in arguments and entangled in the webs of our minds, that we stop growing. With rare exceptions, up until and including the present time in history, this has been the case for all human beings. You can change that. You can raise your children differently. You can honor the wholeness of the being each one of them is, from the beginning.

We need to have a lot of parents raise whole people. We can no longer afford the luxury of waiting for what might naturally evolve over time: a way to not damage all the children so badly. We are in danger of damaging ourselves to death. The problem, formerly serious, has become critical. The sentimental, idealistic romanticism of deeply felt religious belief, though responsible for the suffering of millions, was relatively harmless until we developed hydrogen bombs and many other world-threatening technologies. We can no longer afford to sit around in groups together to indulge in a tearful remembering forward, of a forgotten hoped-for sense of unity, at the direction of various priests and patrolmen who would have us gear up to attack other groups doing the same thing. We must grow beyond where human beings were for all of those years of recalling and hoping for paradise. Because of the various doomsday scenarios for the fate of the earth, we must make a sudden advance in consciousness or perish. Unless more human beings expand who they consider themselves to be, by re-including what they excluded when they grew a personality—unless more of us grow beyond the ignorant provincialism of adolescent moralizing—the game is over. Like rats behind the Pied Piper, we will follow our leader off the cliff and back into the sea forever.

24 ❧ SUMMARY: INTEGRATING THE VOICE OF EXPERIENCE AND A BEGINNER'S MIND

I HAD TO BEGIN RAISING a child when I was nine years old. I paid attention to what was needed because I didn't know what to do exactly. I could also remember, I think, how I had been nurtured so well by my mother and father and sister, before daddy died when I was six and mom went on the bottle. My sister kept loving me until I was nine and she left home. Those three years helped me to remember what my earlier life of being loved and attended to felt like. I didn't have a lot of presumed expertise, which I think helped me learn a lot, not only with my little brother Mike but also with all of my subsequent children. Also, what presumed expertise I gained from that initial experience often got in my way, particularly in the critical way I had of judging my wives and other people's parents. But the degree to which I had what the Buddhist teacher Suzuki called "beginner's mind" I was able to learn from my children. Suzuki said "beginner's mind" was closer to enlightenment than the mind of the expert. I actually think my major skills as a psychotherapist were first developed here, by paying attention to a baby, having to take care of him, not knowing what to do.

What I learned as a ten-year-old parent to my little brother came from (1) paying attention and (2) basing what I did on loving the baby and remembering being loved as a baby. I think that some of the sweetness of people from more peaceful "primitive" cultures is that their memory of how they were nurtured with touch and kindness is kept fresh because they raise their children so close in time to when they were raised and in a community where they still treat each other that way. In a way, everyone with a new baby is in the same boat. That is probably a good thing. If you aren't too smart for your own good, or too culturally brainwashed, or too unfinished with your own parents, that would probably be good enough. All you would have to go on would be your natural instincts and your beginner's mind.

WELCOME

Welcoming the new little being into the world is what we are doing. The new baby enters slowly, reacting with nose, then ears then eyes. Playing with the little discoverer is reassuring and welcoming and invites him out to play. He learns from you to be a little social creature who learns by playing. Warmth and touch games and sound games and smell games and sight games, played slowly and casually and matched to his pace and not imposed upon him, welcome him into the world of human beings who learn by playing games. Playing with him a lot, to invite him into the world of play, is a celebration of the fun of being. This is more important, by far, than getting him into the right pre-school.

When welcoming the new little being into the world of beings, remember what Lewis, Amini and Lannon say about newborns: "Inborn emotionality is undeniable. From the first day out of the womb, some babies are criers, while others lie placid; some are easy to soothe and some inconsolable; some reach for a new rattle, while others shrink away." You pay attention to your unique little being to learn how best to welcome her into her new home in the world. The quality of your parenting is based on paying attention, playing, and loving the child you got.

You want to start out by touching a lot. You communicate mainly through the skin and by variations in balance like rocking, swinging gently, and slow movements back and forth. When the baby gets upset and keeps crying after the diaper is changed and she has enough milk, don't try to make her lie still. When babies are upset, the first thing you want to do to soothe them is not to impose control or shush them up. Join them, don't oppose them. Match their level of energy. If they are yelling at the top of their lungs and flailing, and it is not from a dirty diaper or hunger or a pinch of tape or a diaper pin sticking them, then go for matching their level of activity. Yell like they are and walk around with them and rapidly rock and turn them back and forth to match their same speedy energy and make a noise like the one they are making.

Then, gradually slow it down. Keep walking and rocking back and forth, but slow down more and more. Most of the time, once met where they're at, they will follow you. As your slowing down and their calming down melt into your singing and talking softly, they will continue to respond and become peaceful. Then usually they fall asleep. If you don't wake them up when you put them down, (you may want to keep a little motion going for a while when you put them in their crib by shaking the crib back and forth rhythmically), you can get a chance to sleep a bit yourself. It is great if mom and dad can both do this. The three-way attunement of all three limbic brains is the one of the main great joys of parenting. Besides, coming off a big protest, they are still so endearing and so funny that you can feel good about it even when you are tired.

Sometimes, if something is hurting, like colic, for example, this may not work, or may work just a couple of minutes. However, if the screaming has been escalating, an interruption helps give the child permission to not keep on the kind of panic trail that crying about crying sometimes instigates.

THAT FIRST YEAR

That first year with the first child for most couples is like getting hit by a truck. Many divorces come from the resentment engendered by the demands of child care, which is kind of like having one foot nailed down to the floor. For single moms, the pace and lack of sleep needed to keep up with the baby without some help becomes harder and harder to bear, and it is hard to keep some of it from entering into how the baby is treated. That first couple of years require a lot of attention and effort. For couples, even though both parents can and usually do bond with the baby and love it a lot, not only is the mom feeling overworked and under-rested, but dad isn't getting any sex anymore. The baby owns mom's breasts and her heart and her attention. All men resent this whether they admit it or not.

It is good to have the help of grandparents or a community of friends during this time. If parents don't know how to have arguments and fights, how to be petty and selfish and express it and get over it, they have hell to pay during this time. This is why it takes a village. You need a community of more than the one of you and more than the two of you at this time. Form that community with another parent or set of parents, your own grandparents and other new parents. Take evenings off and let them care for your baby. Take care of their baby sometimes along with yours to give them a break. This is really important.

For the same reasons as above, if you have never learned yoga or meditation this is the time to do that, and to practice what you have learned. Friends who have young children and also do yoga and meditation can be found. Search them out. Share honestly with your mate and your friends how you are doing and what your life is like. You can get and give a lot of help and make this first year wonderful this way. Ask for help from your parents and family and your friends in ways you may not have asked before. Take their gifts of support. They will love the chance to contribute to you and your child.

In that first year, it also helps to pay particular attention to the baby's sense of smell. Babies' sensitivity to smell I think is greater than ours. Familiar smells are comforting and sometimes strong and different smells are upsetting. Just notice what she notices and be sensitive to her sensitivity to senses. Just keep paying attention with empathy. You'll do fine. This has worked with new parents for hundreds of thousands of years.

GIVE YOURSELF A BREAK

For you to do a good job of parenting, you need to carry the baby around with you sometimes while you work, not work too hard, and give yourself a break now and then. It's really important to have short breaks from the baby during the first two years particularly. You need to have time off from childcare for a little while each day, in order to rest and re-center yourself in your own body. Make arrangements with friends or your mate to spell each other now and then. When you feel like you need a break is when you need one. If you can't get one right then, make it the top priority until you get one. When you feel tired, use the baby's nap times to rest instead of work. You can do some work when the baby is awake and carrying the baby while you do is entertaining, educational and fun for you both. You and he are learning "limbic attunement."

LIMBIC ATTUNEMENT

Remember that we have, in evolutionary terms, three brains: the reptilian brain (basic instinct for survival), the limbic brain (the noticing, emotional, intuitive, social-awareness functional brain), and the neocortical brain (thinking and imaging). The first couple of years of parenting are training the attunement of the limbic brain in the child. Remind yourself and your mate and friends of this. Developing the capacity to love in yourself and your child is more important than mere thought. The reptilian brain is hard-wired and doesn't need any training. The limbic brain is learning like a house on fire during those first years of life. You are teaching, and your child is learning, emotionality before she can walk or talk. Here is another charming quote from *A General Theory of Love* for you to think about while you're rocking the baby:

"Infants are early masters of detecting and expressing emotions, which may help to explain their inborn fascination for faces—they have an intrinsic appetite for faces: they look at them, gaze at them, stare at them. But what, exactly are they looking for? Researchers know that babies are looking at the expressions on the faces they fix on. In studying what attracts infant attention, researchers rely on measurements of gaze, because babies will look longer at novel objects than familiar ones. One can demonstrate in this manner that infants just a few days old can distinguish between emotional expressions.

"What is so important to a baby about knowing his mother's emotional state? A scenario called the visual cliff suggests an answer. A baby is placed on a countertop, half solid and half clear Plexiglas. From the baby's point of view, he reaches an abyss when the Plexiglas begins, and he seems in danger of falling. The translucent plastic provides real, albeit invisible support, and thus, the visual cliff presents babies with an ambiguous threat. To an infant unschooled in the nature of Plexiglas, it appears he will fall, but since the surface is solid to the touch, he can't be sure. How does he make sense of it?

"A typical baby crawls to the edge of the cliff, sees the possible precipice, and then looks at his mother—and makes his assessment of the cliff's lethality by reading her expression. If she radiates calm, he continues crawling, but if he finds alarm on her face, the baby stops in his tracks and cries. Whether they realize it or not, mothers use the universal signals of emotion to teach their babies about the world. Because the display is inborn [and universal], emotions not only reach across the gaps between cultures and species, but they also span the developmental chasm between mother and infant. Emotionality gives the two of them common language years before the infant will acquire speech . . . An infant can detect minute temporal changes in emotional responsiveness. This level of sophistication is from an organism that won't be able to stand up on his own for another six months.

"Your baby is attending to you for signals from the very beginning. Those signals you give out are determining the quality of life for her future. Your awareness of your role as reassurer and confirmer that life is okay, and that experimenting to discover things is safe, helps you to parent more powerfully."

I have to stop quoting from this fascinating book now, but again I recommend it to all parents, because the authors' concept of limbic resonance—which they call "a symphony of mutual exchange and internal adaptation whereby two mammals become attuned to each other's inner states"—is awe-inspiring. In the evolutionary story, with the birth of the limbic brain, we began developing a way of sensing what was going on with others of us, which was the beginning of love.

In your baby's interaction with you a very old story is being replayed. As she grows she retraces, in her little individual life, the steps of evolution, and your love of her teaches both of you more than your mind can comprehend. You two are each other's teachers. She learns about love from you from day one.

One of the reasons it is important for you to get a break from the kids now and then is so you can keep giving nurturing, loving signals instead of tired, angry, sad, disturbing signals that develop a mood of upset in the baby. Give yourself and your baby and your community of support a break. Live in constant communication and exchange of help and everything will turn out okay.

DON'T BE FOOLED BY LANGUAGE INTO THINKING YOUR CHILD CAN THINK LIKE YOU

As your child gets older and learns to walk and talk, don't assume that just because she can speak and understand language, she is able to understand abstract principles. Don't preach to her. Don't "should" on her. Love her and listen. Pay attention to find out what she actually does get about the world. Don't assume that it is the same as what you get. Don't forget this attention, and remind the other parents in your life of it often.

Your child already knows how to notice. You can learn more from him than you can teach him about noticing. If you notice how he notices, you can rediscover your own ability to notice, and get your life back from what you learn from your child. There is something irresistibly fascinating about the fascination of a child for whatever is in front of him. This fascination with your child's fascination is a limbic brain phenomenon that is very hard to articulate but nevertheless very real for the parents.

For instance, when you feed your child, just what is it that is so gratifying about your child eating food? It is an intense but ineffable pleasure to watch your child eat and enjoy food. It is very weird to me but I have had other parents tell me the same thing—that we sometimes get more pleasure from watching our children eat than from eating ourselves! One benefit of watching your child eat is that it can teach you how to enjoy food totally. It is a retraining program in concentration and appreciation.

CREATING

Creativity based on what you notice is the key to not being run by your cultural neuroses. Raising children to be creators comes from being a creator yourself and from leaving them alone to follow their natural inclination to create. What frees you to be a creator is the ability to change your identity from your performance (the grades you get, the degrees you got, the titles you have, how much money you make, how good a parent people think you are) to your being (who notices and plays). When your children get noticed by you, and played with lovingly, you have given them the main thing they need.

Raising creators is the idea that allows for transcendence of limited cultural beliefs because it is more fundamentally characteristic of the species, regardless of culture. How we were built, what we are to do in life, is to learn by living. A little human being grows and thrives in a family of caretakers, who have a little less caretaking work to do as each day passes by. As the little being gets incrementally more capable of taking care of herself, acknowledge her for it and be happy. That's your main job.

Learn to meditate and practice it so you can pay better attention to your children. Paying better attention allows you to notice them as they learn and grow in their ability to take care of themselves. Be happy about it. Play with your children every day and relish it, particularly during those first seven or eight years. Good luck. Love those little beings. They are an entryway into loving all of being. Give them my love.

TWELVE RULES OF THUMB

(1) TOUCH YOUR CHILDREN A LOT. Cuddle, snuggle and kiss them a lot. And carry them around with you a lot and hand them off to your mate and other people and other kids to carry around and play with them.

(2) Don't ever try to teach them anything unless they give you a clear indication they want to know something or, after they can talk, they ask.

(3) Consider them to be your teachers who have come to you to remind you of how wise you are from having been loved as a child yourself.

(4) Have a family bed for many years and let your kids sleep with you and your mate until they want to move into another room (maybe as long as seven or eight years old). Don't worry about sex. You will still be able to have sex as much as you like without doing it in front of the kids.

(5) Don't lecture them or put them down with your tone of voice. Don't explain anything whatsoever in any way that exceeds one sentence of not more than five words until after they are eleven years old. After that you can have two sentences.

(6) Tell a lot of stories for fun, but don't tell any stories for moral instruction. Don't do any moralizing whatsoever, and when you do, appologize for it. Scaring children into good behavior, out of fear of you, is a part of your pure inbred cultural ignorance left over from the dark ages in which you were raised. Stop it or we will send out a parenting cop to get you and punish you.

(7) Read stories to them a lot and play a lot of imaginary games with them.

(8) Watch cartoons with them and laugh with them a lot.

(9) Read a lot of children's joke books to them, and later with them. Make a lot of jokes and enjoy their jokes. The most wonderful people in the world are comedians. Most of them are children.

(10) Don't tell them what or when to wear, eat, sleep, urinate, defecate, or drink. They already have a sufficient system for how to discover everything there is to know about all that called the involuntary nervous system. If they get cold they will put clothes on. If they get hungry they will eat. Leave them the hell alone so they can learn from their experience. Support them when they do.

(11) Love them, honor them, laugh with them, enjoy them and love them again.

(12) Pay attention to them and be honest with them. Tell them everything they want to know about your own life, whether you are embarassed or ashamed to, or not. Admit that a lot of times you don't know what to do, and admit it at the very times you don't.

◯‧⁄‥ RADICAL PARENTING
PARTIAL ANNOTATED BIBLIOGRAPHY

ADDITIONAL BOOKS NOT MENTIONED IN THE TEXT BUT SUPPORTIVE OF THE IDEAS PRESENTED IN RADICAL PARENTING

Spirit Matters by Michael Lerner (Walsch Books, 2001).

As the movement for Emancipatory Spirituality becomes more present in the public discourse, more and more parents will realize that their children need the kind of caring that can only be gotten in an atmosphere in which competition and the values of the cutthroat marketplace are not at the center of the educational venture.

Giving the Love that Heals: A Guide for Parents by Harville Hendrix and Helen Hunt (Pocket Books, 1997).

Especially read the section "What an Unconscious Parent Thinks." This is particularly reinforcing of the idea that individuals who are parents need to heal their own wounds from their own childhoods in order not to wound their own children.

It Takes a Village and Other Lessons Children Teach Us by Hillary Rodham Clinton (Simon & Shuster, 1996).

Even though I don't like Hillary much and in my opinion she did little or nothing to actually impact child-rearing practices and the economics of child care when she was in a position to do so, and even though her moralism and self righteousness peeks through, she does have compassion for children and has a heart and is smart and knows how important love for little children is.

When Things Fall Apart: Heart Advice for Difficult Times by Pema Chodron (Shamballa, 1997).

This is about willingness to stay present to suffering and include it all, not avoiding anything, and still keep an open heart. I love Pema Chodron. She speaks of and exemplifies what she calls a "fiercely compassionate attitude."

It Was On Fire When I Lay Down On It by Robert Fulghum (Villard Books, 1990) and *All I Really Need to Know I Learned in Kindergarten* (1988).

This man knows about finding the meaning in life rather than the meaning of life. He knows about love.

Playground Politics: Understanding the Emotional Life of Your School-Age Child by Stanley I. Greenspan, M.D. (Addison Wesley, 1993).

Particularly good about identifying and empathizing with your child's point of view, in order to figure out what is really going on in your family.

(References for other books mentioned are in the text of Radical Parenting)

ʽ✑ PROCLAMATION FOR TRANSFORMING THE LIVES OF CHILDREN

THE FOLLOWING DOCUMENT FROM the Alliance for the Transformation of the Lives of Children, is a source document on everything relevant to staying in touch with the continuum of life with your child. It is a better summation than my own, of the implications of the research and personal experience I have reported on in this book.

WE ENVISION A WORLD WHERE

• Every child is wanted, welcomed, loved, and valued;

• Every family is prepared for and supported in practicing the art and science of nurturing children;

• Adults respect children and honor childhood;

• Children joyfully participate in the life of family and community; and

• Dynamic, resilient, life-honoring cultures flourish.

WE WILL CREATE THIS WORLD BY

• Recognizing that in nature's design there are biological imperatives (ranging from mere physical survival—food, water, air, and shelter—to those that foster optimal human development) that must be fulfilled to support optimal human development;

• Identifying the evidence-linked principles that arise from these imperatives; and

• Acting on these principles that are essential for transforming the lives of children.

CHILDREN ARE IN CRISIS

28%: Pregnant women subjected to physical or emotional violence. (Department of Women's Health, World Health Organization.)
0%: Infant male circumcisions that are medically indicated or beneficial. (American Medical Association, Council on Scientific Affairs.)
85.5%: American infants denied the benefits of breastfeeding for the one-
　　　year minimum recommended by the American Academy of Pediatrics. (Ross Laboratory's Annual Mothers' Survey, 1998.)

25%: Children documented to have been physically struck by age 6 mo.

(Bearing Witness: Violence and Collective Responsibility, Hayworth Press, S.L. Bloom and M. Richert.)

92%: Number of infant and toddler facilities that fail to meet minimum standards.

(University of Colorado, Denver, Economics Department: Cost, quality, and Child outcomes study team.)

40%: Children living apart from biological father.

(US Bureau of the Census, *Current Population Reports,* 1997.)

20%: Children ages 6-12 who have not had a 10-minute conversation with a parent in a month.

(Children's Defense Fund.)

16,000: Number of murders witnessed on TV and computer games by the average child before reaching school age.

(American Medical Association. *Physician Guide to Media Violence,* 1996.)

200%: Increase in suicide, ages 5-14 (5th leading cause of death) since 1979.

(US National Center for Health Statistics, CDC, July 2001.)

9 million: US children under 18 estimated suffering from a psychiatric disorder that compromises their ability to function.

(National Institute of Mental Health)

1.6 million: Number of arrests of children under 18 in US per year.

(US Department of Justice)

5 million: US pre-schoolers living below the poverty line.

(US Bureau of the Census, *Current Population Reports,* 1997.)

"Never before has one generation of American children been less healthy, less cared for, or less prepared for life than their parents were at the same age."

(National Association of State Boards of Education, 1990.)

"Never before has there been such a wealth of information on keeping children healthy, caring for them, and preparing them for life."

(The Alliance for Transforming the Lives of Children, 2001.)

PRINCIPLES FOR TRANSFORMING THE LIVES OF CHILDREN

aTLC's philosophy: Children are innately good, cooperative, and whole in spirit. Parents do the best they can at any given moment, within their present situation and life circumstances. Agreement on a set of guiding principles by all family members promotes enjoyable, confident parenting and provides children with a consistent, supportive environment.

aTLC offers the following evidence-linked Principles for promoting optimal human development. Our deep concern for children and parents is woven into each Principle. We invite you to ponder these Principles that we hope will motivate and inspire you. We encourage you to recognize and follow your intuitive knowledge and instincts. Our intent is to help you co-create with children a life that is practical, harmonious, and joyful.

1. All children are born with inherent physical, emotional, intellectual, and spiritual needs that, when met, foster optimal human development.

Emotional needs for unconditional love, touch, and attention are as valid as physical needs. Responding to crying rather than leaving children alone to "cry it out" shows them that their needs are acknowledged and deepens their basic trust.

2. Every child needs to be securely bonded with at least one other person—optimally the mother.

The infant-mother bond is primary and lays the foundation for all future relationships.

Securing and maintaining a strong bond is the foundation of a parent's effectiveness and the key to a child's optimal development.

3. All children are by nature social beings, born with the drive to play, learn, cooperate with others, and contribute to their world.

Children are more able to reach their full potential when treated with respect within a loving environment that meets their emotional and physical needs, and encourages and supports innate curiosity and spontaneous learning.

Flexibility, clear thinking, age-appropriate problem solving, and intuition are optimized in a child-led learning environment that offers clear, consistent boundaries along with creative, cooperative activities, interaction with nature, unstructured play, and time to simply be.

4. Each child carries within a unique pattern of development designed to unfold in accordance with the child's own rhythm and pace. Every child deserves trust and respect for her or his own emerging learn-

ing styles and abilities. Parents who perceive their child's pattern of development are better able to nurture their child in harmony with this pattern.

5.   Young children communicate their needs through behavior that is strongly influenced by innate temperament, early experiences, the behavior modeled by others, and current circumstances. Children naturally imitate those around them. When adults discover what a child's behavior is actually communicating, they are better able to respond to the need rather than react to the behavior.

6.   The ability of parents and caregivers to nurture children is strongly influenced by their own birth, childhood, and life experiences.

The more adults understand and compensate for their own unmet physical and emotional childhood needs, the better able they are to meet the needs of children in their care.

Once they are better informed, parents who lacked adequate information, resources, or support during the earlier stages of their children's development can strive to compensate for unmet needs.

7.   Children depend upon their parents and caregivers to keep them safe and to protect them from emotional and physical neglect, violence, sexual abuse, and other toxic conditions. Violence, such as infant circumcision, spanking, shaming, and emotional abuse weakens or impairs children's sense of wholeness, trust, and security.

Toxic influences that damage children's brains and nervous systems include over-stimulation from video games, computers, and television, as well as environmental contaminants and behavior-modifying drugs.

8.   A child who is nurtured in the womb of a healthy, loving, and tranquil mother receives the best possible start in life.

The unborn child is a sensitive being who is aware of, and responsive to, the mother's feelings and experience.

A growing life is strongly influenced by the mother's physical, mental, and emotional wellbeing, as well as the quality of support she receives throughout pregnancy.

9.   A natural birth affords significant benefits to mother and baby; therefore, both the potential benefits and risks of any intervention warrant careful consideration.

A natural birth is more likely to occur in an environment based on the midwifery model of care, with physical and emotional support, nourishment, freedom of movement, and individualized attention.

The possible benefits of any contemplated test, procedure, drug, or surgery must be weighed against the immediate and long-term risks, according to current scientific evidence.

10. Breastfeeding, continual physical contact, and being carried on the body are necessary for optimal brain and immune system development, and promote the long-term health of the baby and mother.

Spontaneous breastfeeding for a minimum of two years supports optimal bonding, immunity, and nutrition.

Carrying infants in-arms or wearing them in slings throughout the day provides the near-constant movement that optimizes brain development as well as the touch, safety, and comfort essential to secure bonding.

11. A father's consistent, meaningful, and loving presence in a child's life is significant to the child, father, mother, and the wellbeing of the family.

The father's role may begin with preparation for conception and continues with the physical and emotional protection and support of the mother, baby, and mother-child bond.

In the absence of the biological father, a bonded, ongoing relationship with a loving male caregiver is optimal for every child.

12. Parents create a strong foundation for family life when they consciously conceive, foster, or adopt a child, and are committed to understand and meet the child's needs.

Parents welcome children best when they consciously prepare their own bodies, minds, and spirits for pregnancy and birth, and think of conception as a deep commitment between themselves and the baby.

Even when pregnancy is unplanned, both parents can create a healthy, nurturing environment for their child.

13. Single parents have a special need for a strong emotional and financial support system to effectively nurture their children.

Respecting and supporting a child's healthy relationship with each parent is essential to the child's self-confidence and self-value.

A support system that includes healthy-functioning adults of both genders and multiple generations provides balanced nurturing and role modeling.

14. Political, economic, and social structures either enhance or diminish parents' opportunities to nurture and sustain a secure bond with their children. Support from the immediate community and society at large is crucial if parents are to maintain a secure bond with their children in a nuclear family structure.

Society benefits and families thrive when health care and socio-political structures support all families in preparing for optimal gestation, birth, and parenting.

15. When children live in socially responsive families and communities, they receive a foundation for becoming socially responsible themselves. Children learn to respect and respond to the needs of others when they are seen and heard, and their opinions and needs are recognized, respected, and met.

Engaging children in age-appropriate, creative, and compassionate problem solving and decision-making within the family and the community fosters their becoming responsible members of a society.

16. Effective parenting is an art that can be learned.

Information about children's developmental stages, temperament, and individuality helps parents make informed decisions and serve as advocates of the child's wellbeing. Ready access to evidence-linked information about optimal human development is vital for societies that have departed from nature's biological imperatives.

By implementing these Principles through Actions such as those suggested in the aTLC Blueprint, societies can transform themselves into dynamic, life-honoring cultures where children are loved, protected, respected, valued, and encouraged to joyfully participate in the vital life of family and community.